FROM YOUR
ICE CREAM MAKER

REVISED EDITION

COLEEN AND BOB SIMMO

Bristol Publishing Enterprises

Hayward, California

A **nitty gritty**® Cookbook

©2003 Bristol Publishing Enterprises, Inc., 2714 McCone Ave., Hayward, CA 94545. World rights reserved. No part of this publication may be reproduced in any form, nor may it be stored in a retrieval system, transmitted, or otherwise copied for public or private use without prior written permission from the publisher.

Printed in the United States of America.

ISBN: 1-55867-282-6

Cover design: Frank J. Paredes
Cover photography: John A. Benson
Food stylist: Susan Devaty
Illustrator: James Balkovek

CONTENTS

1   Making Ice Cream: Tips and Techniques
12   Rich and Creamy
54   Light and Luscious
74   Deliciously Low Fat
98   Fat-free
110   Sauces
117   Ice Cream Accompaniments
124   Old-fashioned Soda Fountain Treats
138   Elegant Desserts
152   Index

MAKING ICE CREAM:
TIPS AND TECHNIQUES

Everybody LOVES ice cream! Most people have fond childhood memories of ice cream. For some, it might be a birthday party or a visit to an ice cream parlor for a special occasion. We remember hand-cranked ice cream on Nebraska farms, and ice cream socials put on by local churches as fund-raising events. The ladies would vie to see who could produce the richest ice cream. On the farm, cream and eggs were abundant, and no one was watching their diet. During the fall of late Depression days, just before the start of the Second World War, Bob remembers his family waiting for the horse watering tank to freeze over so his father could take an ax and chop out enough ice to make homemade ice cream.

Now we make ice cream not only because we love the dense, creamy texture, but also because we can be certain of exactly what is in it. Inexpensive commercial ice creams tend to have questionable ingredients added, simply for the purpose of reducing cost or increasing volume. The ice cream you make at home can contain the freshest natural ingredients. Besides, waiting for the ice cream to freeze is much more romantic than just opening a carton, and the anticipation only adds to the enjoyment of opening the ice cream freezer and serving the ice cream.

We include a broad range of frozen dessert recipes and have tried to make each recipe complete, so you don't have to flip pages to follow it. The one exception is the procedure for drained yogurt, which is described in this section. Once you have made it, it will be very easy to do again without looking at the instructions. Most recipes are designed to yield about 1 quart of ice cream. The yield will vary depending on the type of freezer used and the speed of freezing. All mixes expand as they freeze, so a good rule is not to fill a freezer container more than ¾ full.

TYPES OF FROZEN DESSERTS

- Ice cream is dense, rich and creamy. It usually contains cream and eggs or egg yolks.
- Gelato (which is the Italian word for ice cream) contains less air and is a thick, substantial ice cream with more eggs and egg yolks, but less cream.
- Sherbet is less rich than ice cream. It is made with light cream or milk, is usually fruit-flavored and sometimes contains gelatin.
- Frozen yogurt uses yogurt to replace some of the milk or cream, yielding a lower fat dessert with a slight tartness that complements fruit flavors.
- Sorbet does not contain milk. It contains pureed fruit or fruit juices with very intense flavors.

INGREDIENTS

The secret to making great ice cream is to use the highest quality ingredients you can find. As the ice cream melts on the tongue, defects are readily noticeable.

VANILLA EXTRACT

Heading the list is the ubiquitous vanilla extract. Use only the highest quality pure vanilla extract. The cost difference per quart of ice cream is only pennies, but the taste difference is remarkable.

CHOCOLATE AND COCOA

Often unsweetened cocoa is better in chocolate-flavored ice creams than solid chocolate. Buy a high-quality Dutch process cocoa and heat it with the sugar or corn syrup to develop and distribute its full flavor. When you use solid chocolate, be sure to melt it slowly and to combine completely with warm liquid before chilling. This will prevent the chocolate from clumping and leaving little bits of undissolved chocolate in your ice cream. Blending the mix in a blender will help to better combine the chocolate. If you suspect lumps, pass the chilled mix through a fine sieve when you pour it into the freezer container.

SWEETENERS

We prefer to use pure cane sugar to sweeten ice cream. It has received less processing and isn't as likely to have "off" flavors as is sugar derived from beets or other sources. If you are going to assemble the mix in a blender container or food processor workbowl, regular granulated sugar is fine. If you just stir the mix with a spoon, use superfine sugar, which dissolves more easily. In recipes calling for brown sugar, we like dark brown cane sugar. For sherbets and sorbets, we like to use light corn syrup. It produces a nicer texture than granulated sugar. Some recipes call for you to dissolve sugar in water to make a simple syrup: this syrup is slightly sweeter than light corn syrup but doesn't produce quite as nice a texture. Honey can be used, but we find that the flavor dominates other flavoring added to the mix.

We have used NutraSweet, which is the dietetic sweetener found in Equal, in a few recipes. The taste is fine, but the frozen product isn't nearly as smooth as it would be if you used sugar or corn syrup. If your diet restricts sugar intake, ice cream made with NutraSweet makes an acceptable substitute for the real thing.

NUTS

Chopped nuts are wonderful when added to an ice cream mix or sprinkled over frozen ice cream. Buy the freshest nuts available, and if they are not already toasted, put them on a cookie sheet in a 350° oven for a few minutes. Shake the cookie sheet occasionally so they toast evenly. Remove the nuts from the oven when they just begin to release the fragrance of toasted nuts. Allow to cool, and chop coarsely before adding to the almost frozen mix.

EGGS

When we were kids, our parents added raw eggs or egg yolks to ice cream mix without giving it a second thought. With the recent documented cases of salmonella-induced illness, we must now be prudent in the use of raw eggs. Care must even be taken with cooked custard ice cream. The classic "cook until mixture coats the back of a spoon" instructions are not adequate to totally eliminate salmonella problems. The custard must be heated to a temperature of 160° before being chilled, to be free of harmful bacteria. After heating and chilling, the ice cream is smoother than it would have been if it had not been heated.

As with all ingredients, freshness is very important in eggs. Buy your eggs only from a store that does a volume business in eggs and refrigerates them. Always store your eggs in the refrigerator, and buy only the quantity that you will use in a week or 10 days. If an egg is cracked or dirty, discard it.

Fortunately, in recent years several products have come on the market that help alleviate the uncooked egg problem. These are the "egg substitutes," which are pasteurized and, therefore, bacteria-free until opened. They can be added to a mix without cooking and then frozen without concern. Some of these products consist mainly of egg whites and are totally fat-free. Other products replace the yolks with an unsaturated, cholesterol-free fat. The product that we used most in testing these recipes is Egg Beaters. It comes in a convenient 4-ounce container, just the right amount for a 1-quart ice cream recipe, and helps produce a better texture without adding any fat or cholesterol. All the recipes calling for egg substitutes work well with Egg Beaters, but using a substitute that contains fat will produce a richer, creamier ice cream that is higher in calories.

MILK AND CREAM

The fat content of milk and cream varies, not only from region to region, but also from producer to producer within the same region. The most consistent product is nonfat or skim milk, which is legally required to have less than 1/2 percent milk fat, but may have dried milk solids added to give it some body and keep it from looking so "blue" in the glass. Low-fat milk has about 1 percent milk fat and 11 percent milk solids. Reduced fat milk or "two percent ten" has about 2 percent milk fat and 10 percent milk solids. Whole milk has about 3 1/2 percent milk fat and 8 percent milk solids, but this can vary widely depending on the breed of cow, the feed that it receives and the dairy that bottles it. Half-and-half has about 10 percent milk fat. Light cream is next (about 20 percent milk fat), then heavy cream (about 40 percent). Any of the recipes can be made richer by using a richer type of milk or cream, enhancing the texture and creaminess. Conversely, recipes can be made leaner, but you will give up something in texture, and the resulting product will have a more grainy texture.

BUTTERMILK

Before yogurt became commonly available, many homemade ice cream recipes called for buttermilk. Real churned buttermilk has flecks of milk fat and adds richness as well as tartness to a frozen dessert. While neither of us is especially fond of buttermilk as a drink, we do like the taste of ice cream made with buttermilk and have included several recipes that use it. Again, use the buttermilk that you prefer in your ice cream: cultured, churned, with or without some milk fat.

YOGURT

In testing the desserts that call for yogurt and drained yogurt, we used every brand of yogurt available in our local supermarkets. We were amazed at the wide variation in texture, creaminess and acidity. Some were made from whole milk. Others had nonfat dry milk added to skim milk to make a product lower in fat. Some added tapioca or other starch or gelatin to produce a creamier product. The tartness of the yogurts varied widely, and those with "active cultures" seemed to get even more tart as they approached their "use by" dates. Yogurts made from whole milk produce a smoother, creamier frozen dessert, just as frozen desserts made with half-and-half are smoother than those made with plain milk. Let your conscience and dietary restrictions be your guide. Fruit-flavored frozen yogurts are especially delicious. The tartness of the yogurt perks up the flavor of the fruit, eliminating the need to add lemon juice to balance the sweetness. Plain yogurt, whether it is homemade or commercially produced, contains a lot of whey, which is basically just mildly acidic water with a slight bitterness, but it adds little to the character of frozen yogurt.

DRAINED YOGURT

Fortunately, it is very easy to drain much of the whey from yogurt. All you need is a yogurt strainer, which can be inexpensively purchased in housewares departments or gourmet specialty stores. If you don't have a yogurt strainer, the old method of lining a strainer with several layers of damp cheesecloth or a coffee filter works well. In a pinch you can even use an old tea towel or an old T-shirt. After it is drained, yogurt is thicker and will yield a creamier, more nutritious frozen dessert.

Place a pint of plain, natural yogurt, homemade or commercial, in a strainer suspended over a measuring cup or bowl. The yogurt should not contain gelatin or added starch. There should be enough room in the receiving container to hold a cup of liquid without touching the strainer. Cover with an inverted plastic bag and put in the refrigerator for 8 hours or overnight. Depending on the yogurt used, the volume will reduce to about half, or 16 ounces yogurt will yield about 1 cup drained yogurt.

FRUITS AND BERRIES

Nothing is better than seasonal fruits, picked at the peak of perfection. The season is short for most fruits and berries, so find an excuse to make a frozen dessert from them while they are at their finest. If you get a yearning for fresh peach ice cream in February, however, the frozen peach slices that are sold in 16-ounce bags serve as a wonderful substitute for fresh fruit. This is also true for strawberries, raspberries, blackberries, cherries and blueberries. While it is still frozen, the fruit can be placed in a blender container or food processor workbowl along with the remaining ingredients and processed until smooth.

ICE CREAM MAKERS

Old-fashioned hand-cranked ice cream makers are still available, in capacities ranging from 1 quart to several gallons. At least one company makes the same freezer in both hand-cranked and electric models. The more expensive freezers have wooden tubs, which are very durable and offer some insulation for the melting ice. The mix is placed in a freezer can that is immersed in the melting ice. The crank or motor turns the can around a stationary dasher that scrapes the newly frozen mix from the sides of the rotating can. Less expensive models have fiberglass or plastic tubs. All produce a smooth, creamy frozen dessert.

A newer innovation utilizes a sealed, coolant-filled canister that is put in the freezer for at least 8 hours or overnight. When it is very cold, chilled ice cream mix is placed in the container. As the mixture freezes on the sides of the container, it is scraped off by a rotating paddle. This type of freezer is available in both motorized and hand-cranked models. One motorized model will make two one-quart batches at the same time. The ice cream is almost as smooth and creamy as that made in the old-fashioned-type freezer. The most expensive makers have built-in chilling units and one only has to turn on the machine and pour in the chilled mix. This type usually has a capacity of a little over 1 quart. The main advantage of these machines is convenience.

Regardless of the type of machine you use, follow the manufacturer's instructions for freezing frozen desserts

SALT AND ICE

If your ice cream maker uses salt to melt ice, you have some choice as to the type of salt you use. Rock (or "ice cream") salt works best in old-fashioned freezers, but in a pinch you can always use kosher salt or even table salt.

The best ice to use in an old-fashioned freezer is ice crushed in pieces about the size of marbles. Some manufacturers call for ice cubes, which is very convenient if your refrigerator is equipped with an automatic icemaker.

A good rule of thumb is to use 1 part salt to 12 parts ice. We save ½-gallon milk containers, fill them with water and freeze them. When they are solidly frozen it only takes a couple of firm taps with a hammer on each side to shatter the ice into small pieces. You can then pour the crushed ice into the freezer tub. Three ½-gallon containers and a cup of salt are more than enough to make a full quart of frozen dessert.

HELPFUL HINTS

Most recipes containing eggs and cream call for a "dash" of salt which is about ⅛ teaspoon; a "pinch" is about 1/16 teaspoon. Many people are cutting down on their sodium intake, and the salt can be totally omitted if desired. A little salt does pick up the flavor of many frozen desserts, but you should certainly not use more than ¼ teaspoon for a 1-quart frozen dessert recipe.

We found that the frozen fruit juice concentrates, used undiluted, have strong, pure flavors and make easy, economical frozen desserts. Likewise, canned nectars and juices are great basic ingredients. They have a good acid-fruit balance and a strong fruit flavor.

For coffee-flavored desserts, we found that a high quality instant espresso coffee adds a very pleasant coffee flavor eliminating the need of brewing extra strong coffee and allowing it to cool.

We have added liqueurs or other alcoholic beverages to several recipes as they help carry the flavor of the dessert. If you add more than ¼ cup alcohol per quart of mixture, it won't freeze totally and will remain slushy. Triple Sec is especially nice in fruit-flavored desserts but orange juice and a little grated orange peel can be substituted.

We have added nonfat dry milk to many of our recipes. This doesn't add any fat, and helps smooth out the finished dessert. Too much dried milk tends to make the dessert gummy and taste dull. We prefer nonfat dry milk over evaporated milk, which sometimes adds a strange "cooked" taste.

We tend to like frozen desserts that are less sweet than most commercial products, but if you like sweeter desserts, add more sugar or corn syrup. You can also add a packet or two of Equal to the recipe as written. This will make the dessert taste sweeter without adding calories.

We found a heavy duty blender to be very effective in mixing recipes. The ingredients can be added directly to the blender container, blended until thoroughly combined and then placed in the refrigerator to chill in the blender container. Just before pouring into the ice cream freezer, blend for a few seconds to recombine the ingredients and to incorporate a little air into the mixture, which will lighten the ice cream. If you don't have a blender, a food processor works almost as well.

Homemade frozen desserts are at their best when served in chilled dishes straight from the ice cream maker. They will keep for a few days in the freezer, but larger ice crystals develop and the desserts become grainier. Freeze in a plastic microwave-safe container. Freezer stored ice creams tend to get very hard. If they are allowed to mellow in the refrigerator for 30 minutes before serving, they will be softer and more manageable. Or, you can put the container in the microwave for a minute or two on DEFROST. This will make the dessert easier to serve and improve the texture.

You are ready to start making luscious homemade desserts. We have included a wide variety of recipes and hope you will find a few that really please you.

RICH AND CREAMY

14   Almond Praline Ice Cream
15   Almond Praline
16   Chocolate Pecan Praline Ice Cream
17   Easy Caramel Ice Cream
18   Chocolate Orange Ice Cream
19   Hazelnut Gelato
20   Apple Calvados Ice Cream
21   Chocolate Gelato
22   White Chocolate Coconut Gelato
23   Irish Coffee Ice Cream
24   Mocha Almond Fudge Ice Cream
25   Honey Goat Cheese Ice Cream
26   Coffee Ice Cream
27   Dulce de Leche Ice Cream
28   Cognac Ice Cream
29   Two Ginger Ice Cream
30   German's Chocolate Pecan Ice Cream
31   Mexican Chocolate Ice Cream

32	Green Tea (Matcha) Ice Cream
33	Old-fashioned Chocolate Ice Cream
34	Super Chocolate Ice Cream
35	Rocky Road Ice Cream
36	Spicy Avocado Ice Cream
37	Rich Strawberry Ice Cream
38	Rich Butter Pecan Ice Cream
39	Sweet Cherry Ice Cream
40	Chocolate Cherry Ice Cream
42	Old-fashioned Lemon Ice Cream
43	Frozen Zabaglione Ice Cream
44	Chestnut Rum Ice Cream
45	Pistachio Nut Ice Cream
46	Orange Coconut Sherbet
47	Peanut Brittle Ice Cream
48	Creamy Peanut Butter Ice Cream
49	Butterscotch Ice Cream
50	Holiday Eggnog Ice Cream
51	Raspberry Vanilla Swirl Ice Cream
52	Philadelphia-style Vanilla Ice Cream
53	Rich Vanilla Custard Ice Cream

ALMOND PRALINE ICE CREAM

Make Almond Praline, page 15, before you start the ice cream, and crush it into a fine powder. This ice cream is delicious served with some fresh sliced strawberries or peaches.

2¾ cups half-and-half
¼ cup sugar
1 pinch salt
3 eggs

¾ cup *Almond Praline* powder, page 15
2 tsp. vanilla extract
⅛ tsp. almond extract

Combine half-and-half, sugar and salt in a small saucepan. Heat until bubbles start to form around the edge and mixture is quite warm. Whisk eggs in a small bowl. Carefully whisk in a few spoonfuls of hot cream mixture to eggs to gradually warm them. Pour egg mixture back into saucepan and continue to cook over low heat until custard thickens slightly and reaches 160° on a candy thermometer. Remove from heat; pour through a strainer into a small bowl set in another bowl of cold or ice water. Stir in praline powder, vanilla and almond extract. When cool, cover and chill in the refrigerator until ready to freeze. Pour into the ice cream maker and follow the manufacturer's instructions for freezing.

ALMOND PRALINE

Make this ahead of time and keep in an airtight container. Sprinkle it on top of ice cream or sundaes, or use it as an ingredient in ice cream. Substitute chopped pecans for almonds to make Pecan Praline.

1 tsp. vegetable oil
½ cup sugar
2 tbs. water

½ cup blanched slivered almonds or pecans,
  lightly toasted

Lightly coat a cookie sheet or a large piece of foil with vegetable oil. Combine sugar and water in a small heavy saucepan. Cook over medium low heat without stirring until sugar melts and turns a light golden brown. Pour in nuts, tipping saucepan to cover nuts with caramel mixture as much as possible. The caramel mixture will turn dark very quickly, so watch carefully as you continue to cook for another minute or two, just until nuts and syrup turn a dark golden brown. Immediately pour nuts and syrup out on oiled cookie sheet or foil and allow to cool. As soon as praline is cool, break into pieces and process in a food processor workbowl or blender container. If using as a topping, process until pieces are quite small. If adding to an ice cream mixture before freezing, process to a powder. Praline will absorb moisture at room temperature, so store it in an airtight container immediately after crushing.

CHOCOLATE PECAN PRALINE ICE CREAM

Makes about 1 quart

Nuggets of pecan give this luscious chocolate ice cream a little crunch. Make Pecan Praline *by using the recipe for* Almond Praline, *page 15, substituting chopped pecans for almonds. Make it ahead and keep tightly covered.*

1 cup milk
1/3 cup unsweetened cocoa
2 cups half-and-half
1/4 cup dark corn syrup
1/2 cup (4 oz.) Egg Beaters or egg substitute

2 tbs. nonfat dry milk
2 tsp. vanilla extract
1 dash salt
3/4 cup *Pecan Praline*

Heat milk with cocoa in a small saucepan until cocoa dissolves. Remove from heat and place saucepan in a bowl of cold or ice water to cool mixture. Pour into a blender container or food processor workbowl and add remaining ingredients, except *Pecan Praline.* Process until smooth. Cover and refrigerate until ready to freeze. Pour mixture into the ice cream maker, add *Pecan Praline* and follow the manufacturer's instructions for freezing.

EASY CARAMEL ICE CREAM

Leftover caramel ice cream sauce can be used to make a delicious quick ice cream. A drizzle of chocolate sauce adds a nice touch.

³/₄ cup *Caramel Sauce,* page 112
¹/₂ cup (4 oz.) Egg Beaters or egg substitute
2¹/₂ cups half-and-half
¹/₃ cup nonfat dry milk
1 tsp. vanilla extract
1 dash salt

Heat *Caramel Sauce* slightly so it will pour into a blender container or food processor workbowl. Add remaining ingredients and process until smooth. Chill in the refrigerator until ready to freeze. Blend for a few seconds before pouring into the ice cream maker. Follow the manufacturer's instructions for freezing.

CHOCOLATE ORANGE ICE CREAM

Tiny bits of orange peel accent the luscious chocolate flavor of this ice cream.

1 cup whole milk
2 cups heavy cream
1/4 cup sugar
3 oz. bittersweet chocolate, coarsely chopped
2 tbs. unsweetened cocoa

3 egg yolks
1/2 cup orange marmalade
2 tbs. Triple Sec or orange juice
1 tsp. vanilla
1 dash salt

Combine milk and cream in a saucepan and heat over low heat until bubbles form around the edge and mixture is hot. Add sugar, chocolate and cocoa and stir to dissolve.

Beat egg yolks in a small bowl and carefully whisk in a few spoonfuls of hot cream mixture to eggs to gradually warm them. Stir eggs back into saucepan and cook over low heat, stirring constantly, until mixture thickens slightly and reaches 160° on a candy thermometer. Remove from heat and stir in marmalade, Triple Sec, vanilla and salt. Pour into a bowl and place in a pan of ice water. Cool to room temperature. Chill in the refrigerator until ready to freeze. Just before freezing, pour into a blender container and blend for a few seconds. Pour into the ice cream maker and follow the manufacturer's instructions for freezing.

HAZELNUT GELATO

Toast hazelnuts in a shallow pan in a 350° oven for 8 to 9 minutes; remove, place on a heavy towel and rub nuts vigorously in the towel to remove brown skins.

1 cup toasted hazelnuts, as many skins
  removed as possible
2 cups half-and-half
2 eggs
2 egg yolks

2/3 cup dark corn syrup
2 tbs. Frangelico or brandy
1 tbs. vanilla extract
1 dash salt

Process nuts in a food processor workbowl or blender container until very fine. Heat half-and-half in a small saucepan until bubbles form around the edge and mixture is quite warm. Beat eggs and egg yolks together in a small bowl. Carefully whisk in about 1/2 cup of the hot cream mixture, a spoonful at a time, into eggs to gradually warm them. Return eggs to cream in saucepan and continue cooking over low heat, stirring constantly, until mixture forms a custard and reaches 160° on a candy thermometer. Remove saucepan from heat and place in another bowl of cold or ice water to cool mixture to lukewarm. Pour through a strainer into a blender container or food processor workbowl. Add remaining ingredients. Process until smooth. Cover and refrigerate until ready to freeze. Follow the manufacturer's instructions for freezing.

APPLE CALVADOS ICE CREAM

Apples, brandy and cinnamon in this ice cream bring back memories of the best baked apple you have ever eaten. The cooked apples are folded in at the end of freezing.

1 tbs. unsalted butter
2 large Golden Delicious apples, peeled, cored and sliced, about ¾–1 lb.
¼ cup Calvados or other apple brandy
1½ cups half-and-half

1 cup heavy cream
½ cup light brown sugar
1 dash salt
⅓ cup frozen apple juice concentrate
1 tsp. vanilla

In a large skillet, melt butter and sauté apples over medium heat until softened but not browned, about 5 or 6 minutes. Remove from heat and add Calvados. Return to heat and carefully ignite Calvados. When flames die down, remove from heat. With a slotted spoon, remove about ½ cup of the apple mixture. When cool, chop reserved apples into pea-sized chunks and set aside.

In a large saucepan over medium heat, add half-and-half, cream, sugar and salt. Heat slowly to 160°; do not boil. Place pan over a bowl of ice water and stir until cool. Pour cream mixture into a blender container. Add vanilla and remaining apple mixture from skillet; process until thoroughly blended. Refrigerate for at least 4 hours or overnight. Just before freezing, return to blender container and process for a few seconds. Follow the manufacturer's instructions for freezing. Just before ice cream is finished freezing, add reserved chopped apples.

CHOCOLATE GELATO

This Italian-style ice cream is smooth, creamy and very definitely chocolate. Part of the cream is whipped and folded in just before freezing the gelato.

1 tsp. plain unflavored gelatin
1/4 cup cold water
1 1/2 cups half-and-half
1 1/2 cups heavy cream
2 tsp. instant espresso coffee powder

1/2 cup sugar
3 oz. unsweetened chocolate, melted
1 tsp. vanilla extract
1 pinch salt

Soften gelatin in cold water. Heat half-and-half and 1/2 cup cream in a heavy saucepan over low heat until bubbles form around the edge. Do not boil. When cream is hot, sprinkle in coffee; add sugar and gelatin. Stir to dissolve gelatin and remove from heat. Whisk melted chocolate into hot cream; stir in vanilla and salt. Pour mixture through a strainer into a medium-sized bowl. Place bowl in a pan of cold or ice water to cool mixture. Cover and chill in the refrigerator until ready to freeze. Whip remaining heavy cream until thick but not stiff, and gently fold into chilled mixture just before freezing. Pour mixture into the ice cream maker and follow the manufacturer's instructions for freezing.

WHITE CHOCOLATE COCONUT GELATO

Toasted coconut folded into this ice cream adds a terrific flavor crunch.

2$1/2$ cups milk
$1/3$ cup sugar
1 pinch salt
4 oz. white chocolate

3 egg yolks
1 tsp. vanilla extract
$1/2$ cup sweetened flaked coconut, toasted in a
    300° oven for 10-12 minutes

Combine milk, sugar and salt in a heavy saucepan over low heat. Coarsely chop chocolate and add to saucepan. Cook over low heat until chocolate melts. Whisk egg yolks until thick and lemon-colored. Carefully whisk in some of the hot mixture to egg yolks to gradually warm them. Add egg yolks to saucepan and continue to cook over low heat until mixture thickens and reaches 160° on a candy thermometer, about 10 to 12 minutes. Remove from heat and add vanilla. Cool in a bowl of cold or ice water, cover and chill in the refrigerator until ready to freeze. Pour into a blender container or food processor workbowl and process on high for 10 seconds before pouring into the ice cream maker. Follow the manufacturer's instructions for freezing. When gelato is finished, stir in $1/4$ cup toasted coconut. Sprinkle remaining coconut on individual dishes just before serving.

IRISH COFFEE ICE CREAM

This is an appropriate dessert for St. Patrick's Day, or any time for coffee lovers.

1½ cups milk
2 tbs. instant espresso coffee powder
½ cup brown sugar
1¼ cups heavy cream
½ cup (4 oz.) Egg Beaters or egg substitute
2 tsp. vanilla extract
¼ cup Irish whiskey or brandy
1 dash salt

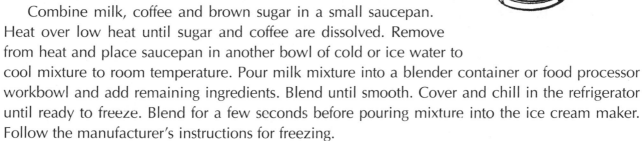

Combine milk, coffee and brown sugar in a small saucepan. Heat over low heat until sugar and coffee are dissolved. Remove from heat and place saucepan in another bowl of cold or ice water to cool mixture to room temperature. Pour milk mixture into a blender container or food processor workbowl and add remaining ingredients. Blend until smooth. Cover and chill in the refrigerator until ready to freeze. Blend for a few seconds before pouring mixture into the ice cream maker. Follow the manufacturer's instructions for freezing.

MOCHA ALMOND FUDGE ICE CREAM

A prepared chocolate fudge topping from the supermarket is folded into this wickedly rich ice cream.

3/4 cup chopped toasted almonds
1 cup milk
1/2 cup (4 oz.) Egg Beaters or egg substitute
2/3 cup sugar
1 tbs. instant espresso coffee powder

1 dash salt
1 1/2 cups heavy cream
1 tsp. vanilla extract
1/2 cup chocolate fudge topping

Toast almonds in a 300° oven until lightly browned. Watch carefully to prevent burning, stirring occasionally. Allow to cool. Place milk, Egg Beaters, sugar, coffee and salt in a blender container or food processor workbowl. Process until well combined. Add cream and vanilla and pulse to combine. Cover and chill in the refrigerator until ready to freeze. Blend on high for a few seconds before pouring into the ice cream maker. Follow the manufacturer's instructions for freezing. When ice cream is frozen, add almonds just before removing from ice cream maker. Remove dasher and make a hole in the ice cream with the handle of a large wooden or metal spoon. Pour in fudge topping and swirl through ice cream with the spoon handle. Do not distribute too evenly: leave some pools of chocolate in the ice cream.

HONEY GOAT CHEESE ICE CREAM

Try one of the unusual, full-flavored honeys such as lavender, mesquite or acacia to flavor this ice cream. Darker, full-flavored honey provides a richer, more dominant flavor.

1 cup heavy cream
1¾ cups half-and-half
2 tbs. sugar
½ cup honey
2 eggs

5 oz. creamy fresh goat cheese, crumbled,
    about ¾ cup
1 tsp. vanilla
1 tbs. lemon juice
1 dash salt

Combine cream and half-and-half in a large saucepan. Heat over low heat until bubbles form around edge and mixture is hot. Add sugar and honey and stir to dissolve.

Beat eggs in a small bowl and carefully whisk in a few spoonfuls of the hot cream mixture to eggs to gradually warm them. Stir eggs back into saucepan and cook over low heat, stirring constantly, until mixture thickens slightly and reaches 160° on a candy thermometer. Remove from heat, strain into a large bowl and whisk in goat cheese. Mix until goat cheese melts. Add vanilla, lemon juice and salt. Place bowl in a pan of ice water and cool to room temperature. Chill in the refrigerator until ready to freeze. Just before freezing, pour into a blender container and blend for a few seconds before pouring into the ice cream maker. Follow the manufacturer's instructions for freezing.

COFFEE ICE CREAM

This is a terrific, creamy, intensely coffee-flavored dessert. Layer it in an ice cream cake or serve it in Cookie Cups, *page 120.*

1 cup whole milk
$^2/_3$ cup sugar
2 egg yolks, lightly beaten
2 tbs. instant espresso coffee powder

1 tsp. vanilla extract
2 cups heavy cream
1 pinch salt

Heat milk in a small saucepan until bubbles form around the edge. Dissolve sugar in heated milk. Remove milk from heat and add 1 to 2 tbs. hot milk to egg yolks to bring eggs gradually up to milk temperature. Add egg-milk mixture and coffee back to saucepan. Continue to cook over low heat, stirring constantly, until mixture begins to thicken and reaches 160° on a candy thermometer. Place saucepan in a pan of cold or ice water and continue stirring to cool custard. When barely warm pour custard through a strainer into a bowl. Stir in vanilla, cream and salt. Chill in the refrigerator until ready to freeze. Pour into the ice cream maker and follow the manufacturer's instructions for freezing.

DULCE DE LECHE ICE CREAM

Dulce de Leche is a South American favorite. Milk and sugar are cooked slowly for hours until the volume is reduced and sugars are caramelized. An acceptable substitute can be made by cooking an unopened can of sweetened condensed milk in simmering water for three hours. This process can be done ahead of time.

1 can (14 oz.) sweetened condensed milk	1 dash salt
1 cup heavy cream	2 egg yolks
1½ cups half-and-half	2 tsp. vanilla
¼ cup superfine sugar	2 tbs. dark rum or bourbon, optional

Place unopened can of condensed milk in a large saucepan with a lid. Add enough water to cover can by 1 inch and bring water to a boil over medium heat. Reduce heat to a bare simmer and cover pot. Simmer for 3 hours. Check occasionally to assure that the can is still well covered with water. The contents will keep for weeks if the can is unopened.

Add cream, sugar and salt to a double boiler and place over simmering water. Stir to combine. In a bowl, whisk egg yolks to combine and stir into cream mixture. Cook to a temperature of 160°. Remove pan from water, strain mixture into a bowl and whisk in canned, cooked dulce de leche, vanilla and rum. Place bowl in a large bowl of ice water. Stir until mixture comes to room temperature. Refrigerate for 4 hours or overnight. Follow the manufacturer's instructions for freezing.

COGNAC ICE CREAM

This is a wonderful finish for a spicy dinner. The ice cream mix should be very cold before you start freezing it, because of the cognac. A dollop of chocolate sauce is a very nice accent.

2 cups heavy cream
1 cup milk
1/2 cup (4 oz.) Egg Beaters or egg substitute
2/3 cup sugar
1 tsp. instant espresso coffee powder
1 tbs. vanilla extract
1/4 cup cognac or brandy

Combine ingredients in a blender container or food processor workbowl. Blend until smooth. Cover and chill in the refrigerator until ready to freeze. Pour into the ice cream maker and follow the manufacturer's instructions for freezing.

TWO GINGER ICE CREAM

The refreshing flavor of fresh ginger is added to the ice cream mix and crushed crystallized ginger is folded into the frozen ice cream at the last moment. Garnish with fresh strawberries or peach slices if you like.

2 cups half-and-half
1 cup heavy cream
1/2 cup peeled, coarsely chopped fresh ginger
3/4 cup light corn syrup

1 tbs. lemon juice
1 tsp. vanilla
1 dash salt
1/4 cup finely chopped crystallized ginger

In a large saucepan, combine half-and-half, heavy cream and ginger. Bring almost to a boil over medium heat. Remove from heat and let stand for 15 to 20 minutes. Mixture may appear curdled, but is fine. Strain cream and ginger mixture into a blender container and discard strained ginger. Add corn syrup, lemon juice, vanilla and salt to cream. Blend for a few seconds to combine. Pour into a bowl and place in a pan of cold or ice water. Stir mixture until it reaches room temperature. Refrigerate until thoroughly chilled. Just before freezing, pour mixture into a blender and blend for a few seconds. Pour blended mixture into the ice cream maker. Follow the manufacturer's instructions for freezing. A minute or two before ice cream is finished, add crystallized ginger.

GERMAN'S CHOCOLATE PECAN ICE CREAM

Makes about 1 quart

The flavors of German's chocolate cake also make a luscious ice cream. Sweetened coconut and chopped pecans add both texture and flavor.

4 oz. Baker's German's chocolate, melted
1 cup half-and-half
1 cup milk
1/3 cup sugar

2 eggs
1 tsp. vanilla extract
1/2 cup sweetened flaked coconut
1/2 cup toasted chopped pecans

Melt chocolate in the microwave on MEDIUM, or in the top of a double boiler. In a medium saucepan over low heat, combine half-and-half, milk and sugar. Cook until bubbles form around the edge and mixture is warm to the touch. Whisk eggs in a small bowl and slowly add several spoonfuls of hot milk mixture to eggs to gradually warm them. Add eggs to saucepan and continue to cook over low heat, stirring constantly. Mixture will thicken slightly and reach a temperature of 160° on a candy thermometer. Stir in warm melted chocolate and vanilla. Place saucepan in a bowl of cold or ice water to cool mixture. Pour through a strainer into a blender, cover and process until well combined. Chill in the refrigerator until ready to freeze. Pour into the ice cream maker and follow the manufacturer's instructions for freezing. Just before ice cream is completely frozen, add coconut and pecans. Mix a little longer to combine ingredients.

MEXICAN CHOCOLATE ICE CREAM

Sweet Mexican chocolate is a blend of chocolate, vanilla, almonds and cinnamon available at Latin American and and specialty stores. Look for the Ibarra brand. The combination of flavors makes a delicious ice cream.

1 round (3.1 oz.) Mexican chocolate, broken into 5–6 pieces
1½ cups half-and-half
1½ cups heavy cream
⅔ cup sugar
1 dash salt

Combine chocolate pieces with remaining ingredients in a small saucepan. Heat over low heat until chocolate and sugar dissolve. Remove from heat; place saucepan in a bowl of cold or ice water to cool. Cover and chill in the refrigerator until ready to freeze. Blend for a few seconds before pouring into the ice cream maker. Follow the manufacturer's instructions for freezing.

VARIATION

Make an ice cream cake alternating layers of *Rich Vanilla Custard Ice Cream,* page 53, *Mexican Chocolate Ice Cream,* page 31, and your favorite cake.

GREEN TEA (MATCHA) ICE CREAM

A traditional Japanese meal doesn't usually end with a sweet or frozen dessert but for the occidental diner Japanese restaurants often feature a green tea ice cream as a dessert. Both the delicious flavor and pale green color are provided by green tea powder, the same as is used in formal Japanese tea ceremonies. This tea can be found in Asian specialty stores and is usually sold in small tins labeled "Matcha" or sometimes "Maccha."

1 cup heavy cream	1 dash salt
2 cups half-and-half	2 tsp. vanilla
2/3 cup sugar	1 tbs. lemon juice
1 tbs. green tea powder	1/2 cup (4 oz.) Egg Beaters or egg substitute

In the top of a double boiler, place heavy cream, half-and-half, sugar, green tea powder and salt. Heat over simmering water and whisk to dissolve sugar and tea. Heat to 160° on a candy thermometer. Remove from heat and whisk in vanilla, lemon juice and Egg Beaters. Cool in a bowl of ice or cold water. When cool, refrigerate for 4 hours or overnight. Just before freezing, place in a blender container and process for a few seconds. Follow the manufacturer's instructions for freezing.

OLD-FASHIONED CHOCOLATE ICE CREAM

Chocolate is one of the world's favorite ice cream flavors.

1 cup milk
2 cups heavy cream
1/2 cup sugar
2 egg yolks, beaten

2 oz. semisweet chocolate, melted
1 oz. unsweetened chocolate, melted
2 tsp. vanilla extract
1 dash salt

Combine milk and cream in a saucepan. Heat over low heat until bubbles form around the edge and mixture is hot. Add sugar and stir to dissolve. Beat egg yolks in a small bowl and carefully whisk in a few spoonfuls of hot cream mixture to eggs to gradually warm them. Stir eggs back into saucepan and continue to cook over low heat, stirring constantly, until mixture thickens slightly and reaches 160° on a candy thermometer. Remove from heat and strain custard into a bowl. Add chocolates, vanilla and salt. Place bowl in a pan of cold or ice water and cool to room temperature. Chill in the refrigerator until ready to freeze. Pour into the ice cream maker and follow the manufacturer's instructions for freezing.

SUPER CHOCOLATE ICE CREAM

This intensely chocolate-flavored ice cream is a family favorite.

¼ cup water
½ cup sugar
2 tbs. unsweetened cocoa
1 dash salt
6 oz. semisweet chocolate chips

3 cups half-and-half
2 tbs. nonfat dry milk
1 tbs. butter
2 tsp. vanilla extract

In the top of a double boiler, over simmering water, combine water, sugar, cocoa and salt. Add chocolate chips and stir to melt. Over low heat in another saucepan, heat half-and-half, dry milk and butter until butter melts and mixture is very warm to the touch. Add to chocolate mixture and continue to cook over low heat until mixture is well combined and smooth. Remove from heat, add vanilla and cool to room temperature. Cover and chill in the refrigerator until ready to freeze. Pour mixture through a strainer into the ice cream maker and follow the manufacturer's instructions for freezing.

ROCKY ROAD ICE CREAM

Add more nuts, marshmallows and chocolate chips if you like your ice cream really rocky.

2 cups heavy cream
1 cup half-and-half
1/3 cup sugar
1 dash salt
6 oz. milk chocolate, melted

1/2 cup (4 oz.) Egg Beaters or egg substitute
2 tsp. vanilla extract
1/2 cup chopped toasted pecans
1/4 cup miniature chocolate chips
1/2 cup miniature marshmallows

Heat cream, half-and-half, sugar and salt in a small saucepan until sugar dissolves. Add melted chocolate and stir to combine. Remove from heat and place in a pan of cold or ice water to cool to room temperature. Strain chocolate mixture into a blender container or food processor workbowl; add Egg Beaters and vanilla. Process until smooth. Chill until ready to freeze. Pour into the ice cream maker and follow the manufacturer's instructions for freezing. About a minute before ice cream is finished, add nuts and chocolate chips and freeze for another minute. When ice cream is frozen, fold in marshmallows.

SPICY AVOCADO ICE CREAM

Makes about 1½ cups

This savory ice cream with avocados, yogurt, and finely chopped jalapeño peppers makes a wonderful float in a cold tomato soup, or use it to crown a tomato and shrimp salad. Garnish with crisp tortilla chips. Remember to drain some yogurt the night before (see page 7).

2 large ripe avocados, peeled, seeded and cut into 6 or 8 pieces
¼ cup half-and-half
¼ cup drained yogurt
¼ cup (2 oz.) Egg Beaters or egg substitute

2 tbs. lime juice
2 tsp. sugar
½ tsp. Tabasco Green Pepper Sauce
½ tsp. salt
1 tbs. seeded, finely chopped jalapeño pepper

In a blender container, combine all ingredients except jalapeño peppers. Process until smooth. Chill in the refrigerator until very cold. Follow manufacturer's instructions for freezing. Just before ice cream is finished, add jalapeño peppers.

As soon as ice cream is frozen, form or scoop into small or medium sized balls, place in a regular or mini-muffin tin or on a chilled plate and put into freezer until hardened. Place in a covered container and store in freezer until ready to serve. If not formed into servings, ice cream can be softened in the microwave on DEFROST for 1 to 2 minutes before serving.

RICH STRAWBERRY ICE CREAM

Here is an old-fashioned, full-flavored strawberry ice cream. Serve a few sweet, sliced strawberries for garnish.

3 cups fresh strawberries, stemmed, or 16 oz. frozen unsweetened strawberries
1½ cups heavy cream
⅔ cup sugar
1 tbs. vanilla extract
2 tbs. Triple Sec or orange-flavored liqueur
1 dash salt

Place strawberries in a blender container or food processor workbowl and puree. Add remaining ingredients and process until smooth. Cover and refrigerate until ready to freeze. Blend for a few seconds before pouring into the ice cream maker. Follow the manufacturer's instructions for freezing.

RICH BUTTER PECAN ICE CREAM

Butter-toasted pecan pieces add great flavor and texture to this ice cream.

3 tbs. unsalted butter
2/3 cup pecans, cut into 1/2-inch pieces
2 cups half-and-half
1 cup heavy cream

1/2 cup sugar
1 dash salt
2 egg yolks
2 tsp. vanilla

In a medium skillet, melt butter over medium heat, add pecan pieces and sauté until lightly browned. Drain pecans through a sieve, reserving butter and pecans. Spoon off as much clear butter as possible, discarding brown bits in bottom of bowl. Combine half-and-half and cream in a large saucepan. Heat over low heat until bubbles form around edge and mixture is hot. Add sugar and salt and stir to dissolve. Beat eggs in a small bowl and carefully add a few spoonfuls of hot cream mixture to eggs to gradually warm them. Stir eggs into saucepan and cook over low heat, stirring constantly, until mixture thickens slightly and reaches 160° on a candy thermometer. Remove from heat, strain into a large bowl and add vanilla and reserved butter. Place bowl in a pan of ice water and cool to room temperature. Chill in the refrigerator until very cold and ready to freeze. Pour into a blender container and blend for a few seconds before pouring into the ice cream freezer. Follow manufacturer's instructions for freezing. About a minute before ice cream is finished, add reserved pecan pieces.

SWEET CHERRY ICE CREAM

Use luscious, fresh, black Bing cherries or frozen, dark, sweet cherries to make this stunning ice cream.

3 cups fresh pitted Bing cherries, or 1 pkg. (16 oz.) frozen pitted dark sweet cherries, defrosted
1/2 cup (4 oz.) Egg Beaters or egg substitute
1 cup half-and-half
2/3 cup superfine sugar
1 dash salt
1 tbs. lemon juice
2 tsp. vanilla extract
1/2 cup heavy cream

Place 2 cups pitted cherries in a blender container or food processor workbowl with Egg Beaters, half-and-half, sugar and salt. Process until smooth. Add lemon juice, vanilla and cream. Process for 2 to 3 seconds until well blended. Chill in the refrigerator until ready to freeze. Coarsely chop remaining cup of cherries by hand. Cover and refrigerate. Pour mixture into the ice cream maker and follow the manufacturer's instructions for freezing. When ice cream is frozen, fold in reserved chopped cherries.

CHOCOLATE CHERRY ICE CREAM

The flavors of a Black Forest cherry cake make a great ice cream. Dried cherries are marinated in Kirsch and added to the ice cream just as it finishes freezing.

1 1/2 cups half-and-half
1 can (12 oz.) evaporated milk
1/2 cup light corn syrup
2 large egg yolks
1 bar (3.5 oz.) good quality bittersweet dark chocolate, melted (prefer Lindt brand)
1 dash salt
1 tsp. vanilla
3 tbs. Kirsch, divided
1/2 cup coarsely chopped dried cherries

In a large saucepan, combine half-and-half and evaporated milk. Heat over low heat until bubbles form around edge and mixture is hot. Add corn syrup and stir to combine.

Beat egg yolks in a small bowl and carefully whisk in a few spoonfuls of hot cream mixture to eggs to warm them. Stir eggs back into saucepan and continue to cook over low heat, stirring constantly, until mixture thickens slightly and reaches 160° on a candy thermometer. Remove from heat, strain into a large bowl, and stir in melted chocolate, salt, vanilla and 1 tbs. of the Kirsch. Place bowl in a pan of cold or ice water and stir until it reaches room temperature. Chill for 4 hours in the refrigerator. While mixture is chilling, gently heat remaining 2 tbs. Kirsch until warm to the touch. Pour over chopped dried cherries. Cover with plastic wrap and reserve. Just before freezing, pour ice cream mixture into a blender container, add any unabsorbed liquid from marinated cherries and blend for a few seconds. Pour into the ice cream maker and follow the manufacturer's instructions for freezing. About a minute before ice cream is frozen, add chopped cherries to mixture.

OLD-FASHIONED LEMON ICE CREAM

Lemon is one of the world's best ice cream flavors. Garnish with fresh mint leaves or raspberries.

1 tsp. grated lemon zest
¼ cup fresh lemon juice
1 cup sugar
½ cup (4 oz.) Egg Beaters or egg substitute
2½ cups half-and-half
1 dash salt

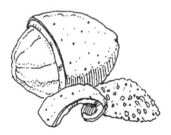

Combine ingredients in a blender container or food processor workbowl and process until smooth. Cover and refrigerate until ready to freeze. Pour into the ice cream maker and follow the manufacturer's instructions for freezing.

FROZEN ZABAGLIONE ICE CREAM

The wonderful flavors of the well-known, frothy, hot, Marsala-laced dessert called zabaglione make a delicious ice cream. Garnish with a few toasted pine nuts or sliced straw-berries, or serve with Zinfandel Syrup, *page 116.*

2½ cups half-and-half
⅔ cup sugar
1 dash salt
3 eggs
¼ cup sweet Marsala

Heat half-and-half, sugar and salt in a saucepan until sugar dissolves and there are bubbles around the edge. The mixture should be quite warm. Whisk eggs in a small bowl and carefully whisk in a few spoonfuls of warm cream to eggs to gradually warm them. Pour eggs into saucepan and continue cooking over low heat, stirring constantly, until mixture starts to thicken and reaches 160° on a candy thermometer. Remove from heat, add Marsala and place saucepan in a pan of cold or ice water to cool mixture. Pour ice cream through a strainer into another bowl, cover and refrigerate until ready to freeze. Pour into the ice cream maker and follow the manufacturer's instructions for freezing.

CHESTNUT RUM ICE CREAM

If you are a chestnut fancier, try this ice cream. The chestnut and rum flavors make a terrific fall or holiday dessert. The chestnut spread is available in the fancy food section of most supermarkets. If only chestnut puree is available, increase the dark corn syrup to ⅔ cup.

1 can (8¾ oz.) chestnut spread
2 tbs. dark corn syrup
2 cups heavy cream
½ cup (4 oz.) Egg Beaters or egg substitute
¼ cup dark rum
1 dash salt

Combine ingredients in a blender container or food processor workbowl and blend until well combined. Cover and chill in the refrigerator until ready to freeze. Blend for a few seconds before pouring into the ice cream maker. Follow the manufacturer's instructions for freezing.

PISTACHIO NUT ICE CREAM

Use unsalted roasted pistachios in this delicately green ice cream. This makes a delicious layer in Rainbow Bombe, *page 151, or in a parfait.*

2 cups half-and-half
1 cup milk
$1/2$ cup (4 oz.) Egg Beaters or egg substitute
$2/3$ cup sugar
2 tsp. vanilla extract
$1/8$ tsp. almond extract
1 dash salt
1–2 drops green food coloring, optional
$1/2$ cup coarsely chopped roasted pistachio nuts

Combine ingredients except pistachios in a blender container or food processor workbowl and process until well combined. Cover and chill in the refrigerator until ready to freeze. Blend for a few seconds before pouring into the ice cream maker. Follow the manufacturer's instructions for freezing. About a minute before ice cream is finished, add nuts and finish freezing.

ORANGE COCONUT SHERBET

Makes about 1 quart

Creamy canned coconut milk is the base for this tropical-flavored sherbet.

1 cup frozen orange juice concentrate, partially defrosted
1 can (14 oz.) coconut milk
1/3 cup light corn syrup
1/2 cup milk
2 tbs. nonfat dry milk
2 tbs. Triple Sec or orange-flavored liqueur
1 dash salt
1/2 cup sweetened flaked coconut

Combine ingredients except coconut in a blender container or food processor workbowl and process until smooth. Cover and chill in the refrigerator until ready to freeze. Add coconut to mixture and blend for a few seconds before pouring into the ice cream maker. Coconut should be coarsely chopped but not smooth. Follow the manufacturer's instructions for freezing.

PEANUT BRITTLE ICE CREAM

Salty, sweet peanuts make a delicious crunch either in or on top of this ice cream. Fold them in just before the ice cream is finished freezing.

2 Snickers® peanut bars (1.4 oz. each), or 3 oz. peanut brittle
3 cups half-and-half
2 tbs. nonfat dry milk
$1/2$ cup (4 oz.) Egg Beaters or egg substitute
$2/3$ cup dark corn syrup
1 tsp. vanilla extract
1 dash salt

Lightly crush candy bars in their wrappers with a rolling pin or small mallet. Remove from wrappers, place in a small bowl and cover so candy doesn't absorb moisture from the air. Combine remaining ingredients in a blender container or food processor workbowl and blend until well combined. Cover and refrigerate until ready to freeze. Blend for a few seconds before pouring into the ice cream maker. Follow the manufacturer's instructions for freezing. About a minute before ice cream is finished freezing, fold in crushed peanut brittle.

CREAMY PEANUT BUTTER ICE CREAM

Makes about 1 quart

This is good straight out of the ice cream maker, or serve it as an ice cream pie in a choco-late cookie crust or Ginger Cookie Crust, *page 142.*

2 cups half-and-half
½ cup milk
½ cup nonfat dry milk
¾ cup peanut butter
¾ cup sugar
2 tsp. vanilla extract

In a medium saucepan, combine half-and-half, milk and dry milk. Cook over low heat to dissolve dry milk. Add peanut butter, stirring until smooth and creamy. Add sugar and cook until dissolved. Remove from heat; add vanilla. Cool mixture in a bowl of cold or ice water before covering and chilling mixture in the refrigerator. Blend for a few seconds before pouring into the ice cream maker. Follow the manufacturer's instructions for freezing.

BUTTERSCOTCH ICE CREAM

This is a luscious, rich, caramel-flavored ice cream.

3 tbs. butter
3/4 cup dark brown sugar
3/4 cup water
1 tsp. instant espresso coffee powder
2 1/4 cups half-and-half
1/4 cup nonfat dry milk
1 1/2 tsp. vanilla extract
1 dash salt

Melt butter in a small saucepan, add sugar and cook over low heat until sugar is dissolved. Add water, bring to a boil, add coffee and simmer for 1 to 2 minutes. Remove from heat and cool in a bowl of cold or ice water. Pour into a blender container or food processor workbowl and add remaining ingredients. Process until smooth. Cover and chill in the refrigerator until ready to freeze. Blend again for a few seconds before pouring into the ice cream maker. Follow the manufacturer's instructions for freezing.

HOLIDAY EGGNOG ICE CREAM

Makes about 1 quart

If you like eggnog, you will love this spicy, creamy ice cream. To make this easiest-ever ice cream, use eggnog straight out of the dairy case and flavor it with brandy, rum or whatever you like in eggnog. For an elegant dessert, use this for a layer in Rainbow Bombe, *page 151.*

3 cups cold eggnog
2 tbs. brandy
generous amount grated nutmeg

Combine ingredients, pour into the ice cream maker and follow the manufacturer's instructions for freezing.

RASPBERRY VANILLA SWIRL ICE CREAM

Make the Raspberry Sauce, *page 113, ahead of time for this easy and pretty dessert. If you prefer, just spoon the sauce over rather than folding it into the ice cream.*

2 cups half-and-half
1 cup milk
²/₃ cup sugar
¹/₂ cup nonfat dry milk

1 tbs. vanilla extract
¹/₈ tsp. lemon extract
1 dash salt
¹/₂–²/₃ cup *Raspberry Sauce,* page 113

Combine ingredients except *Raspberry Sauce* in a blender container or food processor work-bowl and process until mixture is smooth. Cover and chill in the refrigerator until ready to freeze. Pour into the ice cream maker and follow the manufacturer's instructions for freezing. Ice cream should be quite firm when it is frozen; if necessary, put it in the freezer to set up for about 30 minutes. Spoon ice cream out into a chilled bowl. Make a hole in the center of the ice cream with a thick spoon or spatula handle and pour in *Raspberry Sauce.* Starting at the center of the *Raspberry Sauce,* make a circle in the ice cream, dragging it into a swirl. Serve immediately.

PHILADELPHIA-STYLE VANILLA ICE CREAM

Makes about 1 quart

This is a classic vanilla ice cream that doesn't use eggs. If you have a 4- to 5-inch piece of vanilla bean, scrape the seeds into the cream mixture for a delicious flavor. Place the used vanilla bean in a small jar, cover with sugar and keep it in the cupboard. Use the sugar for making desserts.

1 cup heavy cream
2 cups half-and-half
seeds from a vanilla bean, or 1 tbs. vanilla extract
²/₃ cup sugar
1 dash salt

Combine ingredients in a blender container or food processor workbowl until sugar dissolves. Chill in the refrigerator until ready to freeze. Pour into the ice cream maker and follow the manufacturer's instructions for freezing.

RICH VANILLA CUSTARD ICE CREAM

Vanilla ice cream is always a favorite, and this is an elegant, creamy version.

1 cup whole milk
1/2 cup sugar
1 dash salt
2 egg yolks, lightly beaten
2 cups heavy cream
2 tsp. vanilla extract

Place milk in a small saucepan and heat over low heat until bubbles form around the edge and mixture is hot. Add sugar and salt and stir to dissolve. Remove milk from heat and add 1 to 2 tbs. hot milk to egg yolks, mixing well. Continue to add a little more milk to egg yolks to bring eggs gradually up to milk temperature. Add egg-milk mixture back to saucepan and continue to cook over low heat, stirring constantly until it starts to thicken and reaches 160° on a candy thermometer, about 10 to 12 minutes. Place saucepan in a bowl of cold or ice water and continue stirring to cool down custard. When custard is just barely warm, stir in cream and vanilla. Cover and chill in the refrigerator until ready to freeze. Pour mixture through a strainer into the ice cream maker and follow the manufacturer's instructions for freezing.

LIGHT AND LUSCIOUS

55 Blackberry Rhubarb Ice Cream
56 Dried Cherry Ice Cream
57 Fresh Peach Ice Cream
58 Papaya Ginger Sherbet
59 Tangerine Buttermilk Ice Cream
60 Honey Almond Ice Cream
61 Orange Walnut Ice Cream
62 Lemon Cheesecake Ice Cream
63 Quince Apple Dairy-free Sherbet
64 Lemon Tea Ice Cream

65 Pineapple Ginger Ice Cream
66 Cinnamon Candy Ice Cream
67 Cream Sherry Ice Cream
68 Creamy Chocolate Frozen Yogurt
69 Easy Chocolate Malted Ice Cream
70 Spicy Pumpkin Ice Cream
71 Pumpkin Pecan Ice Cream
72 Vanilla Frozen Yogurt
73 Banana Nut Ice Cream

BLACKBERRY RHUBARB ICE CREAM

This intensely flavored ice cream is made with either fresh or frozen, unsweetened black-berries and cooked rhubarb. It takes time to strain the blackberries, but it is worth the effort to get a smooth ice cream. Pair scoops of this with orange sherbet and vanilla ice cream.

1/2 cup water
1/2 cup sugar
8 oz. rhubarb, trimmed and cut into 1-inch pieces
16 oz. blackberries, fresh or defrosted

1 cup heavy cream
2 tbs. nonfat dry milk
1/4 cup crème de cassis
1 dash salt

Combine water and sugar in a small saucepan and bring to a boil. Cook for 2 to 3 minutes until sugar is dissolved. Add rhubarb, cover and simmer for 3 to 4 minutes until fruit is tender. Remove saucepan from heat and place in a pan of cold or ice water to cool mixture. Puree blackberries in a blender container or food processor workbowl with a little cream until smooth. Pour through a coarse strainer and press fruit through the sieve. Discard seeds. Return puree to blender container or food processor workbowl; add remaining ingredients and process until smooth. Cover and refrigerate until ready to freeze. Pour into the ice cream maker and follow the manufacturer's instructions for freezing.

DRIED CHERRY ICE CREAM

Small, tart, dried cherries add a great flavor punch to this kirsch-flavored ice cream.

2½ cups half-and-half
½ cup (4 oz.) Egg Beaters or egg substitute
½ cup sugar
1 dash salt
1 tbs. vanilla extract
2 tbs. kirsch or orange-flavored liqueur
¾ cup coarsely chopped dried cherries, divided

Combine half-and-half, Egg Beaters, sugar, salt, vanilla, kirsch and ¼ cup dried cherries in a blender container or food processor workbowl. Process until sugar is dissolved and mixture is smooth. Cover and chill in the refrigerator until ready to freeze. Pour into the ice cream maker and follow the manufacturer's instructions for freezing. About a minute before ice cream is frozen, add remaining ½ cup cherries to mixture and freeze for another minute.

FRESH PEACH ICE CREAM

Fresh, perfectly ripe summer peaches make a wonderful ice cream. If fresh peaches aren't available, substitute frozen sliced peaches. When serving, sprinkle with some fresh raspberries for color and flavor contrast.

1½ cups half-and-half
¾ cup sugar
¼ cup nonfat dry milk
3 cups peeled pitted sliced peaches, or 1 pkg. (16 oz.) frozen sliced peaches, defrosted
3 tbs. lemon juice
2 tsp. vanilla extract
1 dash salt

Combine half-and-half, sugar and dry milk in a blender container or food processor workbowl and process until smooth. Add peaches with remaining ingredients and process until smooth. Chill in the refrigerator until ready to freeze. Blend mixture for a few seconds before pouring into the ice cream maker. Follow the manufacturer's instructions for freezing.

PAPAYA GINGER SHERBET

Tropical flavors of papaya, ginger, lime and mint are combined in this tasty sherbet. Remember to start draining the yogurt the night before.

2 cups peeled papaya, cut into 1-inch pieces, about 12 oz.
¾ cup half-and-half
¾ cup drained yogurt
½ cup superfine sugar
¼ cup (2 oz.) Egg Beaters or egg substitute
zest of 1 lime
¼ cup lime juice
2 tsp. peeled, grated fresh ginger
1 dash salt
1 tsp. finely chopped mint

Combine all ingredients in a blender container and process on high until mixture is smooth. Chill in the refrigerator for 4 hours or overnight. Just before freezing, pour mixture into a blender container and blend for a few seconds before pouring into the ice cream freezer. Follow manufacturer's instructions for freezing.

TANGERINE BUTTERMILK ICE CREAM

Makes about 1 quart

Fresh tangerine juice makes a pretty, light orange ice cream. This is particularly nice paired with Raspberry Sherbet, *page 76, or a chocolate ice cream in* Cookie Cups, *page 120.*

1 cup fresh tangerine juice (about 1¼ lb. before juicing)
1 cup buttermilk
1½ cups half-and-half
⅓ cup sugar
1 tbs. lemon juice
2 tbs. Triple Sec or orange-flavored liqueur
1 dash salt

Combine ingredients in a blender container or food processor workbowl and blend until smooth. Cover and chill in the refrigerator until ready to freeze. Blend for a few seconds before pouring into the ice cream maker. Follow the manufacturer's instructions for freezing.

HONEY ALMOND ICE CREAM

Makes about 1 quart

The flavor of honey really comes through in this ice cream. Use your favorite kind of honey. Very distinctive types produce a more pronounced honey taste.

2 cups half-and-half
1 cup milk
1/3 cup nonfat dry milk
1/2 cup (4 oz.) Egg Beaters or egg substitute
1/2 cup honey
1 tsp. vanilla extract
1/8 tsp. almond extract
1 dash salt
1/2 cup toasted slivered almonds

Combine ingredients except almonds in a blender container or food processor workbowl. Blend until smooth. Cover and chill in the refrigerator until ready to freeze. Blend for a few seconds before pouring into the ice cream maker. Follow the manufacturer's instructions for freezing. Either fold nuts into ice cream mixture about a minute before ice cream is done and continue to freeze for another minute, or sprinkle them over individual ice cream servings.

ORANGE WALNUT ICE CREAM

Toasted walnuts are folded into this creamy ice cream at the very end of the freezing operation. Serve in Lace Cookies, page 122, made into cookie cups, or make an ice cream pie with a chocolate cookie crust.

1/2 cup frozen orange juice concentrate, partially defrosted	2 tbs. Triple Sec or orange-flavored liqueur
1 cup buttermilk	2 tbs. nonfat dry milk
2 cups half-and-half	1 dash salt
1/2 cup light corn syrup	1/2 cup toasted chopped walnuts

Combine all ingredients except nuts in a blender container or food processor workbowl and process until well combined. Cover and refrigerate until ready to freeze. Blend for a few seconds before pouring into the ice cream maker. Follow the manufacturer's instructions for freezing. About a minute before ice cream is frozen, add nuts and finish freezing.

VARIATIONS

Substitute 1/2 cup toasted flaked coconut for walnuts.

Substitute 1/2 cup chopped dates that have been soaked in 2 tbs. triple sec or orange juice, for the walnuts.

LEMON CHEESECAKE ICE CREAM

Makes about 1 quart

If you like cheesecake, this ice cream is for you. Fresh strawberries or raspberries make a delicious and pretty garnish. This makes an elegant ice cream pie with either a chocolate cookie crust or Graham Cracker Cookie Crust, *page 143.*

2 cups milk
1 pkg. (8 oz.) light cream cheese (Neufchâtel)
1/2 cup sugar
3 tbs. Triple Sec or orange-flavored liqueur

1 tsp. vanilla extract
1/2 tsp. lemon extract
1 dash salt

Place all ingredients in a blender container or food processor workbowl and process until very smooth. Chill until ready to freeze. Pour into the ice cream maker and follow the manufacturer's instructions for freezing.

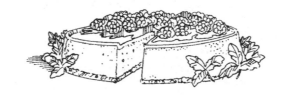

QUINCE APPLE DAIRY-FREE SHERBET

Spain and Mexico produce a prepared quince paste called membrillo which provides a complex accent to the apple flavors in this easy sherbet. Commercially prepared mocha mix is used for the sherbet base.

$1/2$ cup quince paste (membrillo)
$1/2$ cup frozen apple juice concentrate, defrosted, undiluted
3 tbs. light corn syrup
$2^3/4$ cups mocha mix
2 tbs. lemon juice
1 tsp. vanilla
1 dash salt

Place all ingredients in a blender container and process on high for 15 to 20 seconds until mixture is well combined. Chill in blender container in the refrigerator until very cold. Just before freezing, blend the mix for a few seconds and pour into the ice cream maker. Follow manufacturer's instructions for freezing.

LEMON TEA ICE CREAM

Makes about 1 quart

This is a refreshing, lemon-flavored ice cream to serve after a summer lunch. Garnish with a few fresh mint leaves.

3 cups half-and-half
½ cup sugar
6 lemon tea bags
½ cup (4 oz.) Egg Beaters or egg substitute
1 dash salt

In a small saucepan, bring 1 cup half-and-half and sugar almost to a boil. Add tea bags, cover, remove from heat and allow to steep for about 20 minutes. Remove tea bags, pressing out as much liquid as possible. Place pan in a bowl of cold or ice water to cool mixture to room temperature. When tea mixture has cooled, pour into a blender container or food processor workbowl. Add remaining half-and-half, Egg Beaters and salt. Process for a few seconds until smooth. Cover and chill until ready to freeze. Pour into the ice cream maker and follow the manufacturer's instructions for freezing.

PINEAPPLE GINGER ICE CREAM

Fresh ginger adds a delightful flavor to this pineapple ice cream.

1/3 cup water
1/2 cup sugar
1 tbs. finely chopped peeled ginger root
1 cup frozen pineapple juice concentrate,
　defrosted
1 cup half-and-half
1 1/2 cups buttermilk
1/2 tsp. grated lemon zest
1 dash salt

Combine water, sugar and ginger in a small saucepan. Bring to a boil and cook for 3 to 4 minutes until sugar is dissolved and ginger releases its flavor. Place saucepan in a bowl of cold or ice water to cool mixture to room temperature. Strain sugar and ginger mixture into a blender container or food processor workbowl. Add remaining ingredients and blend until smooth. Cover and chill until ready to freeze. Pour into the ice cream maker and follow the manufacturer's instructions for freezing.

CINNAMON CANDY ICE CREAM

Little cinnamon Red Hots make a gorgeous pink, spicy cinnamon ice cream. Make it for your valentine or for a child's birthday party.

1 cup whole milk
¾ cup sugar
¼ cup (2 oz.) Red Hots or cinnamon candies
1 dash salt
2 cups half-and-half
½ cup nonfat dry milk
1½ tsp. vanilla extract

Place milk, sugar, Red Hots and salt in a small heavy saucepan. Cook over low heat, stirring constantly until candies melt, about 10 to 12 minutes. Remove from heat. Place in a bowl of cold or ice water and allow to cool to room temperature. Pour candy mixture into a blender container or food processor workbowl with half-and-half, dry milk and vanilla. Process until smooth. Chill in the refrigerator until ready to freeze. Blend for a few seconds before pouring mixture into the ice cream maker. Follow the manufacturer's instructions for freezing.

CREAM SHERRY ICE CREAM

Sherry is a fortified wine originally from southern Spain. It comes in varieties from dry to sweet. Sweet cream sherry makes a subtly flavored ice cream. Top with toasted pecans or almonds for a crunchy texture.

$3/4$ cup cream or golden sherry
$1/3$ cup dark corn syrup
$1/2$ cup (4 oz.) Egg Beaters or egg substitute
$1/4$ cup nonfat dry milk
2 cups half-and-half
2 tsp. vanilla extract
1 pinch grated nutmeg
1 dash salt

Combine ingredients in a blender container or food processor workbowl and blend until well combined. Cover and chill in the refrigerator until ready to freeze. Blend for a few seconds before pouring into the ice cream maker. Follow the manufacturer's instructions for freezing.

CREAMY CHOCOLATE FROZEN YOGURT

Makes about 1 quart

This tangy dessert is for chocolate lovers!

¾ cup whole milk
1 tsp. plain gelatin
⅔ cup sugar
1 dash salt
2 oz. semisweet chocolate, coarsely chopped
2½ cups plain yogurt
2 tsp. vanilla extract

Place milk in a small saucepan. Soften gelatin in milk. Slowly heat milk to dissolve gelatin. Add sugar, salt and chocolate. Stir over low heat until smooth, but do not boil. Remove from heat and place saucepan in a pan of cold or ice water to cool, or allow to cool at room temperature. Whisk in yogurt and vanilla. Chill mixture in the refrigerator until ready to freeze. Blend for a few seconds before pouring through a strainer into the ice cream maker. Follow the manufacturer's instructions for freezing.

EASY CHOCOLATE MALTED ICE CREAM

Makes about 1 quart

One burger place in Southern California used to serve a thick, wonderful malted ice cream like this in tall, silver malt cups with long spoons.

1 small can (5.5 oz.) Hershey's Chocolate Syrup
2½ cups half-and-half
½ cup (4 oz.) Egg Beaters or egg substitute
⅓ cup malted milk powder
¼ cup sugar
1 dash salt
1 tsp. vanilla extract

Combine chocolate syrup, half-and-half and Egg Beaters in a blender. Process until well mixed. Add remaining ingredients and blend until milk powder and sugar are dissolved. Chill in the refrigerator until ready to freeze. Blend for a few seconds before pouring into the ice cream maker. Follow the manufacturer's instructions for freezing.

SPICY PUMPKIN ICE CREAM

This ice cream has all the wonderful flavors of a good pumpkin pie. Serve it with sugar cookies, or use to fill a Ginger Cookie Crust, *page 142.*

½ cup canned or cooked pumpkin
½ cup (4 oz.) Egg Beaters or egg substitute
½ cup sugar
¼ cup brown sugar
½ cup nonfat dry milk
2 cups half-and-half
¼ tsp. cinnamon
¼ tsp. ground ginger
⅛ tsp. grated nutmeg
1 dash salt

Combine all ingredients in a blender container or food processor workbowl. Process until smooth. Chill in the refrigerator until ready to freeze. Pour mixture through a strainer into the ice cream maker and follow the manufacturer's instructions for freezing.

PUMPKIN PECAN ICE CREAM

Pumpkin, pecans and a little rum make a great fall dessert. Try building alternate layers with ginger cookie crumbs and Caramel Sauce, *page 112, in a parfait glass..*

1 cup half-and-half
1 cup heavy cream
1 cup canned pumpkin
$1/2$ cup nonfat dry milk
$2/3$ cup dark corn syrup

3 tbs. dark rum
2 tsp. vanilla extract
$1/2$ tsp. allspice
1 dash salt
$3/4$ cup toasted chopped pecans

Combine half-and-half, cream and pumpkin in a blender container or food processor work-bowl. Process until smooth. Add remaining ingredients except pecans and process until well combined. Chill in the refrigerator until ready to freeze. Blend for a few seconds before pouring into the ice cream maker. Follow the manufacturer's instructions for freezing. A minute or two before ice cream is frozen, add nuts and continue freezing for another minute to combine ingredients.

VANILLA FROZEN YOGURT

Drain some yogurt the night before making this ice cream (see page 7). This is delicious with any fresh sliced fruit or raspberries.

1 cup drained yogurt
1 cup half-and-half
1 cup milk
2/3 cup sugar
1/2 cup (4 oz.) Egg Beaters or egg substitute
1 tbs. vanilla extract
1 dash salt

Combine ingredients in a blender container or food processor workbowl and blend until smooth. Cover and chill in the refrigerator until ready to freeze. Blend mixture for a few seconds before pouring into the ice cream maker. Follow the manufacturer's instructions for freezing.

BANANA NUT ICE CREAM

Use really ripe bananas to bring out the most intense, sweet banana flavor in this ice cream.

2 large or 3 small very ripe bananas, slightly mashed (about 1½ cups)
2 cups half-and-half
⅓ cup sugar
2 tbs. lemon juice
1 tsp. vanilla extract
1 dash salt
½ cup toasted chopped pecans, walnuts or almonds

Place bananas, half-and-half and sugar in a blender container or food processor workbowl. Process on HIGH until very smooth. Stir in lemon juice, vanilla and salt. Process to combine. Chill in the refrigerator until ready to freeze. Blend for a few seconds before pouring into the ice cream maker. Follow the manufacturer's instructions for freezing. A minute or two before ice cream is frozen, add the nuts and continue to freeze for another minute to combine ingredients.

DELICIOUSLY LOW FAT

75 Strawberry Balsamic Sorbet
76 Raspberry Sherbet
77 Rum Raisin Dairy-free Ice Cream
78 Blueberry Sherbet
79 Fresh Pineapple Sorbet
80 Prune and Brandy Frozen Yogurt
81 Blackberry Frozen Yogurt
82 Strawberry Rhubarb Frozen Yogurt
83 Strawberry Frozen Yogurt
84 Dried Peach Sorbet
85 Dried Apricot Frozen Yogurt
86 Kiwi Orange Sherbet

87 Apple Cinnamon Sherbet
88 Mango Orange Sherbet
89 Gazpacho Ice
90 Savory Carrot Freeze
91 Pineapple Sherbet
92 Banana Daiquiri Sherbet
93 Bittersweet Chocolate Mocha Sorbet
94 Sugar-free Chocolate Ice Cream
95 Chocolate Buttermilk Ice Cream
96 Mocha Sherbet
97 Maple Pecan Ice Cream

STRAWBERRY BALSAMIC SORBET

This light, creamy sorbet goes together quickly and can be made any time of the year using frozen, sweetened strawberries. The balsamic vinegar and black pepper accent the sweet strawberries.

1 pkg. (16 oz.) frozen, sweetened sliced strawberries
1/4 cup (2 oz.) Egg Beaters or egg substitute
2 tbs. balsamic vinegar
1/4 tsp. freshly ground black pepper
1 dash salt

Defrost strawberries until they are slushy and place in a blender container or food processor workbowl with remaining ingredients. Process until smooth. If not freezing immediately, chill in the refrigerator. Pour into the ice cream container and follow the manufacturer's instructions for freezing.

RASPBERRY SHERBET

This beautiful deep-colored sherbet has a light touch of orange flavoring. For a quick dessert, place a scoop of sherbet in a pretty dessert bowl and pour a little Asti Spumante sparkling sweet jjßwine over it.

²/₃ cup water

²/₃ cup sugar

2 pkg. (12 oz. pkg.) unsweetened frozen
    raspberries, defrosted

¹/₂ cup drained yogurt

2 tbs. Triple Sec or orange juice

1 dash salt

In a small saucepan, combine water and sugar. Bring to a boil, lower heat and simmer for 3 to 4 minutes to dissolve sugar. Remove from heat and place saucepan in a large bowl of cold or ice water to cool. Transfer to a blender container, add defrosted berries and process until smooth. Strain through a coarse sieve and discard seeds. There will be about 3 cups of fruit mixture. Combine fruit and remaining ingredients in a blender container and process until smooth. Chill in the refrigerator until very cold. Just before freezing, blend for a few seconds more. Pour into the ice cream maker and follow the manufacturer's instructions for freezing.

RUM RAISIN DAIRY FREE ICE CREAM

You will hardly know from the rich creamy texture that there is almost no fat in this cold, smooth frozen rice pudding.

3 cups unflavored rice milk (prefer Rice Dream)
1/2 cup long grain (not converted) rice
1 dash salt
1 pinch freshly grated nutmeg
1/2 cup sugar

1/2 cup (4 oz.) Egg Beaters or egg substitute
1 tbs. lemon juice
1 tsp. vanilla
1/3 cup dark raisins
3 tbs. dark rum

In a tall saucepan, bring rice milk to a boil. Add rice and salt and stir to combine. When mixture returns to a boil, cover and reduce heat to a bare simmer. Simmer for 30 minutes. Remove from heat, stir in sugar and nutmeg and allow to cool for 10 minutes.

Pour rice mixture into a blender container and process on high until smooth. Add Egg Beaters, lemon juice and vanilla and process for a few seconds. Chill in the refrigerator for at least 4 hours. While ice cream is chilling, combine raisins and rum in a small bowl; cover and marinate. If there is any liquid remaining on the raisins, add to ice cream mixture before freezing. Follow manufacturer's instructions for freezing. Just before ice cream is finished, add raisins and continue freezing for a minute or two to distribute them evenly.

BLUEBERRY SHERBET

Pair this with a scoop each of Raspberry Sherbet, *page 76, and vanilla ice cream for a patriotic holiday dessert.*

1 pkg. (16 oz.) frozen blueberries, partially defrosted, or 2 cups fresh blueberries, stemmed and
   washed
1½ cups milk
¾ cup light corn syrup
3 tbs. lime juice
2 tbs. Triple Sec or orange-flavored liqueur

Combine blueberries, milk, corn syrup and lime juice in a blender container or food processor workbowl. Process until smooth. Pour mixture through a strainer, pressing out all juice. Discard skins. Add Triple Sec to strained mixture, cover and refrigerate until ready to freeze. Pour into the ice cream maker and follow the manufacturer's instructions for freezing.

FRESH PINEAPPLE SORBET

The honey gold pineapples from Hawaii or Central America are worth seeking out as they are incredibly sweet and flavorful. The prepared fresh pineapple chunks available in many supermarkets make this sorbet very easy to put together.

3 cups fresh pineapple pieces, 1 inch pieces
1/2 cup light corn syrup
1/4 cup (2 oz.) Egg Beaters or egg substitute
1 dash salt

Place pineapple in a blender container or food processor workbowl. Add corn syrup, Egg Beaters and salt. Process mixture on high until quite smooth. Refrigerate until well chilled. When ready to freeze sorbet, blend for a few seconds and then pour into the ice cream freezer. Follow manufacturer's instructions for freezing.

PRUNE AND BRANDY FROZEN YOGURT

Sweet dried prunes make a luscious, creamy, low-fat dessert. If the prunes are very hard and dry, simmer them in the heated milk for 15 to 20 minutes before blending.

1 1/2 cups whole milk
1/2 cup nonfat dry milk
1/3 cup sugar
3/4 cup soft pitted prunes, cut into 1/2-inch pieces
2 tbs. brandy or cognac, optional
1 tsp. vanilla extract
1 1/2 cups plain yogurt
1 dash salt

Pour milks and sugar in a blender container or food processor workbowl. Process until well mixed. Add prunes and process on HIGH until smooth. Add remaining ingredients, blending until well combined. Chill in a blender container or food processor workbowl in the refrigerator until ready to freeze. Blend for a few seconds before pouring mixture into the ice cream freezer. Follow the manufacturer's instructions for freezing.

BLACKBERRY FROZEN YOGURT

Fresh or frozen blackberries make a beautiful, dark, creamy yogurt. The drained yogurt (see page 7) makes all the difference in this dessert. Make it the night before; it will also keep for several days in the refrigerator.

1 pkg. (16 oz.) frozen blackberries, defrosted, or 3 cups fresh blackberries, stemmed and washed
1/3 cup sugar
1/3 cup water

1 cup low fat or skim milk
1 cup drained yogurt
1/2 cup nonfat dry milk
2 tbs. black currant liqueur or Triple Sec or orange juice

Process blackberries in a blender container or food processor workbowl. Place in a strainer and push through juice and fruit, discarding seeds. In a small saucepan, combine sugar and water. Bring to a boil, lower heat and cook for 3 to 4 minutes to dissolve sugar. Remove from heat and allow to cool, or place saucepan in a larger bowl of cold or ice water. Combine cooled sugar mixture, blackberry puree and remaining ingredients in a blender container or food processor workbowl. Process until smooth and creamy. Chill in the refrigerator until ready to freeze. Blend for a few seconds before pouring into the ice cream maker. Follow the manufacturer's instructions for freezing.

STRAWBERRY RHUBARB FROZEN YOGURT

Strawberries and rhubarb are a wonderful springtime combination. Garnish with fresh sliced strawberries. Start draining the yogurt the night before making this dessert (see page 7).

$^2/_3$ cup water
$^2/_3$ cup sugar
$^1/_2$ lb. fresh rhubarb, trimmed, cut into 1-inch pieces
1 pt. fresh strawberries, stemmed and washed
3 tbs. nonfat dry milk
$^1/_2$ cup half-and-half
1 cup drained yogurt
1 dash salt

Combine water and sugar in a small saucepan. Bring to a boil, add rhubarb pieces, cover and simmer for 3 to 4 minutes until rhubarb is tender. Cool slightly. Place strawberries in a blender container or food processor workbowl and process until smooth. Add cooled rhubarb and remaining ingredients. Process until smooth. Cover and refrigerate until ready to freeze. Pour into the ice cream maker and follow the manufacturer's instructions for freezing.

STRAWBERRY FROZEN YOGURT

Use fresh or unsweetened frozen strawberries to make this low calorie dessert. Remember to drain the yogurt a few hours before making this dessert, or the night before (see page 7).

1 cup drained yogurt
2½–3 cups fresh sliced strawberries, or 1 pkg. (16 oz.) frozen strawberries, partially defrosted
½ cup nonfat milk
1 tsp. unflavored gelatin, softened in 1 tbs. cold water
1 tbs. nonfat dry milk
2 tbs. NutraSweet sweetener
1 dash salt

Combine yogurt and strawberries in a blender container or food processor workbowl and blend for a few seconds to combine. Heat milk in a small saucepan. Add softened gelatin and stir to dissolve. Add milk, dry milk and NutraSweet to blender. Process until smooth and creamy. Cover and chill until ready to freeze. Pour into the ice cream maker and follow the manufacturer's instructions for freezing.

DRIED PEACH SORBET

Many fruits are dried for the consumer today, and dried peaches are particularly flavorful. Try this refreshing low calorie, icy peach dessert.

10 oz. (about 2 cups) dried peaches
2½ cups water
1 tbs. lemon juice
1 tsp. vanilla extract
⅔ cup superfine sugar
1 pinch grated nutmeg

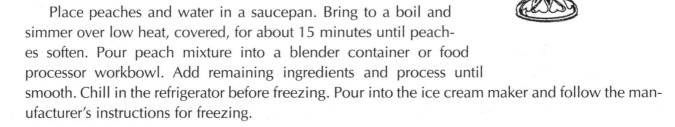

Place peaches and water in a saucepan. Bring to a boil and simmer over low heat, covered, for about 15 minutes until peaches soften. Pour peach mixture into a blender container or food processor workbowl. Add remaining ingredients and process until smooth. Chill in the refrigerator before freezing. Pour into the ice cream maker and follow the manufacturer's instructions for freezing.

DRIED APRICOT FROZEN YOGURT

Dried apricots are available year-round and make a great tangy, fruit-flavored dessert.

$^3/_4$ cup (about 5 oz.) dried apricots
$^1/_2$ cup water
$^1/_2$ cup light corn syrup
2 tbs. lemon juice
$^1/_2$ cup nonfat dry milk
1 cup low-fat milk
$^1/_4$ tsp. almond extract
1 cup nonfat yogurt

Combine apricots and water in a small saucepan. Bring liquid to a boil, cover and simmer for about 15 minutes, until apricots are soft. Remove from heat; allow to cool to room temperature. Pour apricots and liquid into a blender container or food processor workbowl and process until smooth. Add corn syrup, lemon juice, milks, almond extract and salt. Process until well combined. Stir in yogurt and chill in the refrigerator until ready to freeze. Pour into the ice cream maker and follow the manufacturer's instructions for freezing.

KIWI ORANGE SHERBET

The small, brown kiwi has a wide distribution now that it is grown in the United States. Kiwis feel fairly firm even when quite ripe and have a delicious tart flavor.

3 kiwis
1/2 tsp. grated orange peel
1/2 cup orange juice
1 3/4 cups milk
3 tbs. nonfat dry milk
2/3 cup light corn syrup
1–2 drops green food coloring, optional

Cut out the small, hard cores on the stem end of the kiwis and discard. Peel and cut each kiwi into 8 pieces. Place kiwis, orange peel and juice in a blender container or food processor workbowl and process until smooth. Add remaining ingredients and process until well combined. Cover and chill in the refrigerator until ready to freeze. Follow the manufacturer's instructions for freezing.

APPLE CINNAMON SHERBET

The creamy texture and slightly spicy flavors make this a fabulous finale for a fall or holiday dinner.

1 1/4 cups milk
1/2 cup superfine sugar
1/2 cup nonfat dry milk
2 tbs. lemon juice
2 cups canned smooth applesauce
1/4 tsp. cinnamon
1 tsp. vanilla extract
1 pinch each ground nutmeg, ground cloves and
  salt

Pour milk, sugar, dry milk and lemon juice into a blender container or food processor workbowl. Process on HIGH until well mixed. Add remaining ingredients and blend for another 30 seconds. Chill mixture in the refrigerator until ready to freeze. Pour mixture into the ice cream maker and follow the manufacturer's instructions for freezing.

MANGO ORANGE SHERBET

This is a delicious fruit dessert when made with ripe mangoes. Frozen mango chunks also work well. Mangoes have long fibers, so straining the fruit mixture makes a smoother sherbet.

1/2 cup sugar

1/2 cup water

2 large mangoes

1 tbs. lemon juice

1/2 cup frozen orange juice concentrate

1 cup whole milk

1/4 cup nonfat dry milk

1 dash salt

Combine sugar and water in a small saucepan. Bring to a boil, reduce heat and simmer for about 5 minutes. Remove from heat and allow to cool to room temperature. Wash mangoes and peel. Cut fruit away from the flat seed while holding over a bowl to catch juice. Cut all mango pulp from seeds and scoop out from skins with a spoon. You should have about 1 cup fruit and juice. Place mango, lemon juice and orange juice concentrate in a blender container or food processor workbowl. Process on HIGH for 15 to 20 seconds, scrape down sides of bowl and process until smooth, about 45 seconds. Add cooled sugar-water and remaining ingredients; process for another 10 to 15 seconds. Pour mango mixture through a strainer into a bowl or freezer container; place in the refrigerator to chill until ready to freeze. Pour into the ice cream maker and follow the manufacturer's instructions for freezing.

GAZPACHO ICE

Serve this in small goblets. As soon as ice is frozen, form or scoop into balls, place on a cold plate and put in the freezer until ready to serve. Hardened balls can be softened in the microwave on DEFROST for 1 to 2 minutes, or put in the food processor to break up the ice crystals.

2 cups spicy tomato juice
1 large peeled seeded chopped fresh ripe
    tomato
1 cup peeled seeded chopped cucumber
1/4 cup finely minced red onion
1/4 cup finely minced peeled green or red
    pepper

1/2 cup (4 oz.) Egg Beaters or egg substitute
2 tbs. sugar
2 tbs. full-flavored olive oil
2 tbs. red wine vinegar
salt and freshly ground pepper

Combine ingredients in a food processor or blender and pulse 5 or 6 times to combine ingredients but obtain a coarse texture. Cover and chill until ready to freeze. Pour into the ice cream maker and follow the manufacturer's instructions for freezing.

SAVORY CARROT FREEZE

Makes about 1½ cups

Serve small scoops of this vibrant orange ice as a refreshing appetizer on a hot summer evening (or float a scoop in a bowl of chilled vichyssoise). This recipe can be doubled if you are serving more than 4 or 5 plates.

½ lb. carrots, peeled and thinly sliced
1 can (14½ oz.) chicken broth
1 tbs. chopped onion
2 quarter-sized pieces ginger root, peeled and
  grated

1 tbs. balsamic vinegar
2 tbs. frozen orange juice concentrate,
  partially defrosted
salt to taste
generous amount white pepper

Combine carrots, chicken broth, onion and ginger in a small saucepan. Bring to a boil, lower heat, cover and cook for about 20 minutes until carrots and onion are very soft. Remove from heat and allow to cool to room temperature. Place carrots in a blender container or food processor workbowl and add remaining ingredients. Blend until smooth. Adjust seasoning as needed. Cover and chill until ready to freeze. Pour into the ice cream maker and follow the manufacturer's instructions for freezing. Place in the freezer a few minutes after freezing to set up for easier serving. Scoop out small portions just before serving.

PINEAPPLE SHERBET

This is a year-round favorite. All you need is a couple of cans of crushed pineapple on the pantry shelf. This makes a great ice cream pie with a chocolate crust.

2 cans (8 oz. each) crushed unsweetened pineapple with juice
2/3 cup light corn syrup
1 1/2 cups milk
2 tbs. Triple Sec or orange juice

Pour pineapple with juice and remaining ingredients in a blender container or food processor workbowl. Process until smooth. Chill in the refrigerator until ready to freeze. Pour mixture through a coarse strainer into the ice cream maker. Follow the manufacturer's instructions for freezing.

BANANA DAIQUIRI SHERBET

Tropical flavors of banana, lime and rum make an easy summer dessert. The riper the bananas, the better. Coarsely chopped macadamia nuts sprinkled over each serving add a nice touch.

2 cups milk
1 cup (about 2 large) mashed ripe bananas
$1/2$ cup corn syrup
$1/3$ cup nonfat dry milk
$1/2$ tsp. grated lime peel
$1/4$ cup lime juice
2 tbs. dark rum
1 dash salt

Combine ingredients in a blender container or food processor workbowl and blend until smooth. Cover and chill in the refrigerator until ready to freeze. Blend for a few seconds before pouring into the ice cream maker. Follow the manufacturer's instructions for freezing.

BITTERSWEET CHOCOLATE MOCHA SORBET

This is marvelous on its own or paired with a scoop of vanilla or Butterscotch Ice Cream, *page 49.*

6 oz. bittersweet chocolate, melted
1 tbs. vegetable oil
2½ cups water
¼ cup sugar
2 tbs. instant espresso coffee powder
½ cup light corn syrup
1 tsp. vanilla extract
1 dash salt

Melt chocolate in a microwave on MEDIUM or in the top of a double boiler. Stir in oil when chocolate is completely melted and smooth. In a small saucepan, bring water and sugar to a boil and cook for 2 to 3 minutes to dissolve sugar. Stir in coffee. Combine warm melted chocolate with hot water mixture and mix well. Pour into a blender; add corn syrup, vanilla and salt. Blend well. Allow to cool to room tempreature and chill in the refrigerator until ready to freeze. Blend for a few seconds before pouring into the ice cream maker. Follow the manufacturer's instructions for freezing.

SUGAR-FREE CHOCOLATE ICE CREAM

This is a sweet treat for those watching calories and sugar intake.

1 tsp. plain gelatin
2½ cups low-fat milk
½ cup Nestlé Quik Sugar Free chocolate drink mix
1 cup drained yogurt (see page 7)
1 tsp. vanilla extract
1 dash salt

Soften gelatin in ½ cup of the milk. Heat in a small saucepan until gelatin dissolves. Remove from heat and place saucepan in another bowl of cold or ice water to cool mixture to room temperature. Pour mixture into a blender container or food processor workbowl. Add remaining milk, Quik, yogurt, vanilla and salt. Blend until smooth. Cover and chill in the refrigerator until ready to freeze. Blend for a few seconds before pouring into the ice cream maker. Follow the manufacturer's instructions for freezing.

CHOCOLATE BUTTERMILK ICE CREAM

Here is a tangy, low calorie chocolate ice cream.

1½ cups milk
⅓ cup unsweetened cocoa
½ cup sugar
1 tsp. instant espresso coffee powder
2 cups buttermilk
3 tbs. nonfat dry milk
2 tsp. vanilla extract
1 dash salt

Combine ½ cup milk, cocoa, sugar and coffee in a small saucepan. Heat until sugar melts and ingredients are well combined. Remove from heat and place saucepan in another bowl of cold or ice water to cool to room temperature. Pour mixture into a blender container or food processor workbowl and add remaining ingredients. Process until smooth. Cover and chill in the refrigerator until ready to freeze. Blend for a few seconds before pouring into the ice cream maker. Follow the manufacturer's instructions for freezing.

MOCHA SHERBET

This deep coffee-flavored sherbet makes a wonderful dessert for a rich dinner.

3 cups milk
2 tbs. instant espresso coffee powder
1 tbs. unsweetened cocoa
½ cup nonfat dry milk
⅔ cup dark corn syrup
2 tsp. vanilla extract
1 pinch grated nutmeg
1 dash salt

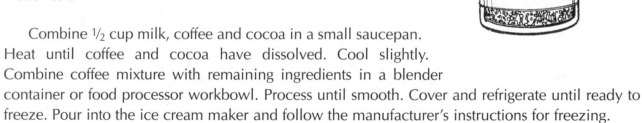

Combine ½ cup milk, coffee and cocoa in a small saucepan. Heat until coffee and cocoa have dissolved. Cool slightly. Combine coffee mixture with remaining ingredients in a blender container or food processor workbowl. Process until smooth. Cover and refrigerate until ready to freeze. Pour into the ice cream maker and follow the manufacturer's instructions for freezing.

MAPLE PECAN ICE CREAM

Toasted pecans accent the delicious maple syrup flavor in this ice cream.

$^1/_2$ cup coarsely chopped toasted pecans
$^1/_2$ cup (4 oz.) Egg Beaters or egg substitute
$^3/_4$ cup maple syrup
2 cups buttermilk
1 cup milk
2 tbs. nonfat dry milk
2 tsp. vanilla extract
1 dash salt

Lightly toast pecans in a 350° oven and set aside to cool. Combine all ingredients except pecans in a blender container or food processor workbowl. Process until well combined. Cover and refrigerate until ready to freeze. Blend for a few seconds before pouring into the ice cream maker. Follow the manufacturer's instructions for freezing. About a minute before ice cream is frozen, add nuts.

FAT-FREE

99   Apple Juice Sorbet

100   Blood Orange Sorbet

101   Cranberry Orange Sorbet

102   Dried Pear Sorbet

103   Fresh Plum Sorbet

104   Orange Spiced Tea Sherbet

105   Pink Grapefruit Sorbet

106   Rhubarb Sherbet

107   Strawberry Daiquiri Ice

108   Strawberry Guava Nectar Sherbet

109   Watermelon Sorbet

APPLE JUICE SORBET

This nonfat easy sorbet starts with frozen apple juice concentrate.

1 can (12 oz.) frozen apple juice concentrate, partially defrosted
2 cups water
2 tbs. lemon juice
1/3 cup light corn syrup
1 dash salt

Place ingredients in a blender container or food processor workbowl and process until smooth. Chill in the refrigerator until ready to freeze. Pour into the ice cream maker and follow the manufacturer's instructions for freezing.

BLOOD ORANGE SORBET

The gorgeous, red-juiced blood oranges make a beautiful and delicious sorbet.

3 cups blood orange juice
1 cup sugar
1/2 cup (4 oz.) Egg Beaters or egg substitute
2 tbs. Triple Sec or orange-flavored liqueur, optional
1 dash salt
finely grated zest of 1 orange for garnish

Combine all ingredients except orange zest in a blender container or food processor workbowl and process until well combined. Cover and refrigerate until ready to freeze. Pour mixture into the ice cream maker and follow the manufacturer's instructions for freezing. Garnish individual servings of sorbet with a little orange zest.

CRANBERRY ORANGE SORBET

This makes an attractive, delicious and low calorie finale for an autumn or holiday dinner. Serve alone or spoon over custard sauce and accompany with some crisp, thin cookies.

8 oz. fresh cranberries, washed and stemmed
1 cup sugar
2 cups water
2 tbs. frozen orange juice concentrate
1 pkg. unflavored gelatin, dissolved in 1/4 cup cold water
1 dash salt

Combine cranberries, sugar, water and orange juice in a medium saucepan. Bring to a boil and simmer for about 10 minutes until cranberries soften and split open. Remove from heat and stir in dissolved gelatin and salt. Cool to room temperature. Pour into a blender container or food processor workbowl and process until smooth. Chill in the refrigerator until ready to freeze. Pour through a strainer into the ice cream maker and follow the manufacturer's instructions for freezing.

DRIED PEAR SORBET

Sorbets satisfy the sweet tooth without adding fat or many calories. Dried fruits make a perfect base for intensely flavored sorbets and ices.

2½ cups water
½ cup sugar
8 oz. (about 1½ cups) dried pears
¼ cup lime juice
1 dash salt

Combine water with sugar and dried pears in a saucepan. Bring to a boil. Reduce heat, cover and simmer for 15 minutes until pears soften. Let cool slightly and pour into a blender container or food processor workbowl with lime juice and salt. Process until smooth. Chill in the refrigerator before freezing. Blend mixture for a few seconds before pouring into the ice cream maker. Follow the manufacturer's instructions for freezing.

FRESH PLUM SORBET

Ripe, juicy plums make a light and pretty dessert sorbet.

1 1/4 cups sugar
1 cup water
1-inch piece cinnamon stick
3 1/2–4 cups halved, pitted red plums
2 tbs. lemon juice
1/2 tsp. vanilla
1 dash salt

In a 2- to 3-quart saucepan, combine sugar, water and cinnamon stick. Bring to a boil over high heat, stirring until sugar dissolves. Add plums and continue boiling, uncovered, for 2 minutes. Cover, reduce heat and simmer for 8 to 10 minutes or until plums are very tender. Remove plums from heat and discard cinnamon stick. Cool slightly; pour plum mixture into a food processor work-bowl or blender container and process until smooth. Stir in lemon juice, vanilla and salt. Cover and refrigerate until thoroughly chilled. Pour into the ice cream maker and follow the manufacturer's instructions for freezing.

ORANGE SPICED TEA SHERBET

Makes about 1 qt.

Constant Comment tea flavors this low-calorie dessert.

½ cup sugar
3 cups milk
4 Constant Comment tea bags
¼ cup nonfat dry milk
½ cup (4 oz.) Egg Beaters or egg substitute
1 dash salt

Combine sugar and 1 cup of the milk in a small saucepan. Bring almost to a boil, add tea bags, cover and steep for about 20 minutes. Pour mixture through a strainer into a blender container or food processor workbowl, pressing out as much liquid from tea bags as possible. Add remaining ingredients and process until smooth. Cover and chill in the refrigerator until ready to freeze. Pour into the ice cream maker and follow the manufacturer's instructions for freezing.

PINK GRAPEFRUIT SORBET

This is a refreshingly tart, year-round dessert. If you use regular frozen grapefruit juice concentrate, increase the corn syrup to ¾ cup.

1 can (6 oz.) frozen pink grapefruit juice concentrate, partially defrosted
2¼ cups water
½ cup corn syrup
1 dash salt

Combine ingredients in a blender container or food processor workbowl. Blend until smooth. Cover and refrigerate until ready to freeze. Pour into the ice cream maker and follow the manufacturer's instructions for freezing.

RHUBARB SHERBET

This lovely pink, slightly tart sherbet makes a refreshing springtime dessert. Sliced or pureed fresh strawberries are a delicious accompaniment.

3/4 cup water
3/4 cup sugar
1 lb. rhubarb, cut into 1-inch pieces
2/3 cup nonfat dry milk
2/3 cup orange juice
2 tbs. Triple Sec or orange-flavored liqueur

Bring water and sugar to a boil in a medium saucepan , lower heat and simmer for 3 to 4 minutes until sugar is dissolved. Add rhubarb pieces, cover and cook over low heat for about 5 minutes, until rhubarb is soft. Remove from heat, uncover and allow to cool to room temperature. Pour rhubarb into a blender container or food processor workbowl, add remaining ingredients and process until smooth. Chill in the refrigerator until ready to freeze. Pour into the ice cream maker and follow the manufacturer's instructions for freezing.

STRAWBERRY DAIQUIRI ICE

Frozen drink mixes make a terrific base for frozen desserts.

²/₃ cup frozen strawberry daiquiri mix, defrosted, undiluted
1³/₄ cups water
¹/₄ cup light rum or orange juice
1 pkg (16 oz.) frozen strawberries, defrosted, or 2 cups sliced fresh strawberries
1 dash salt

Place all ingredients in a blender container or food processor workbowl and blend until smooth. Cover and chill until ready to freeze. Pour into the ice cream maker and follow the manufacturer's instructions for freezing.

STRAWBERRY GUAVA NECTAR SHERBET

The fresh fruit flavors of strawberry and guava make a nonfat, low sodium and totally delicious sherbet.

2 cans (11½ oz. each) strawberry guava nectar
½ cup nonfat dry milk
2 tbs. lemon juice
¼ cup sugar
1 dash salt
fresh strawberry slices for garnish

Place all ingredients except strawberry slices in a blender container. Process on high until smooth. Chill in the refrigerator until ready to freeze. Pour into the ice cream maker and follow the manufacturer's instructions for freezing. Garnish with a few fresh strawberry slices or serve with *Lemon Almond Biscotti,* page 119.

WATERMELON SORBET

This refreshing sorbet is a pretty pink color and really tastes like watermelon. It does take a little time to remove the seeds.

4½–5 lb. piece watermelon
½ cup sugar
⅔ cup water

½ cup (4 oz.) Egg Beaters or egg substitute
2 tbs. lemon juice
1 dash salt

Remove watermelon pulp from rind and scrape out seeds, saving as much juice as possible. Cut watermelon into small chunks and place in a blender container or food processor workbowl. Process until smooth. Strain through a coarse sieve to remove any small white seeds. There should be about 3 cups melon juice. Return melon juice to blender. Combine sugar and water in a small saucepan . Bring to a boil and cook for 3 to 4 minutes, until sugar is completely dissolved. Remove from heat and place pan in a bowl of ice water to cool mixture. Add to melon juice along with remaining ingredients. Process until smooth. Cover and chill in the refrigerator until ready to freeze. Blend for a few seconds before pouring into the ice cream maker. Follow the manufacturer's instructions for freezing.

SAUCES

111 Butterscotch Sauce

111 Apricot Sauce

112 Caramel Sauce

113 Quick Caramel Sauce

113 Raspberry Sauce

114 Blueberry Sauce

115 Mexican Chocolate Sauce

116 Zinfandel Syrup

Some people like their ice cream plain, but it is always tempting to embellish a good thing with a flavorful sauce or a fresh fruit garnish. Ice cream is a perfect foil for your favorite gooey concoction. Sauces can be hot, cold or in between.

Try topping a wonderful homemade vanilla ice cream with a hot caramel sauce, or try a bittersweet chocolate sauce over a lighter chocolate ice cream.

Make some fresh fruit sauces when peaches, strawberries, raspberries and blueberries are in season. The ripe, sweet fruit adds a delicious accent. Try pairing a fresh peach sauce with vanilla ice cream and fresh raspberries, or make *Raspberry Sauce,* page 113, to serve with fresh peach ice cream. Lemon ice cream and blueberries make a wonderful combination. Vanilla ice cream with a fresh strawberry sauce and ripe raspberries is a classic treat.

BUTTERSCOTCH SAUCE

This is a delicious sundae topping. Add a sprinkle of nuts, too, if the occasion demands.

½ cup dark corn syrup
¼ cup brown sugar
¼ cup sugar
¼ cup half-and-half

1 tbs. butter
1 dash salt
1 tsp. vanilla extract

Combine all ingredients except vanilla in a small saucepan. Bring mixture to a full boil. Cook for 5 minutes. Remove from heat and add vanilla. Serve warm.

APRICOT SAUCE

This simple sauce complements a variety of ice creams. Add a few toasted almonds also.

½ cup apricot jam
½ cup canned apricot nectar

1 tbs. brandy or orange-flavored liqueur

Combine jam and nectar in a small saucepan. Bring to a boil, lower heat and cook for 5 to 6 minutes, until jam dissolves. Remove from heat, add brandy and cool to room temperature or refrigerate until ready to serve.

CARAMEL SAUCE

This is a traditional caramel sauce that can be made ahead and reheated in the microwave just before serving.

1 cup sugar
1 cup half-and-half
1 tbs. butter
1 dash salt
¼ tsp. vanilla extract

Place sugar in a heavy 10-inch skillet. Stir with a fork over low heat until sugar melts and turns a golden brown. Remove from heat and slowly pour half-and-half down side of skillet, being careful to keep your hand away from the steam. Sugar will form a big ball. Free sugar from bottom of skillet with fork and return to heat. Stir to dissolve. When sauce is smooth, remove from heat and stir in butter and salt. Allow to cool slightly and stir in vanilla. Serve hot over your favorite ice cream.

QUICK CARAMEL SAUCE

Makes 1¼ cups

This is an easy and delicious ice cream sauce. You can also use some of it to make Easy Caramel Ice Cream, *page 17. Reheat in the microwave.*

½ lb. caramels   ½ cup milk

Place caramels and milk in a heavy saucepan. Stir slowly over low heat until caramels melt and make a smooth sauce. Serve warm.

RASPBERRY SAUCE

Makes about ⅔ cup

A package of frozen raspberries makes a gorgeous full-flavored ice cream sauce.

1 pkg. (12 oz.) frozen raspberries, defrosted   2 tbs. Triple Sec or orange juice
3 tbs. sugar

Combine ingredients in a blender container or food processor workbowl and process until smooth. Pour through a strainer, pushing through as much fruit and liquid as possible. Discard seeds. Refrigerate until ready to serve.

BLUEBERRY SAUCE

Serve this vibrant blue sauce over lemon, orange or strawberry ice cream. The berries add a nice texture. Double the sauce if you need more servings.

$\frac{1}{2}$ cup water
$\frac{1}{3}$ cup sugar
2 tbs. lemon juice
1 tsp. cornstarch
1 tbs. Triple Sec or orange-flavored liqueur
1 cup fresh or frozen blueberries, washed and stemmed

Combine $\frac{1}{2}$ cup water and sugar in a small saucepan. Bring to a boil to dissolve sugar. Add lemon juice. Dissolve cornstarch in Triple Sec. Add to water-sugar mixture and cook over low heat for 1 to 2 minutes until blueberries have softened, sauce thickens slightly and turns clear. Stir blueberries into sauce and heat through. Serve warm or chilled.

MEXICAN CHOCOLATE SAUCE

This cinnamon-almond chocolate sauce can be served hot or cold over ice cream.

1 round (3.1 oz.) store-bought Mexican (Ibarra) chocolate, broken into pieces
½ cup heavy cream
1 tbs. brandy or dark rum

Heat chocolate and cream together over low heat until chocolate melts and mixture is smooth and creamy. Stir in brandy. Refrigerate if not serving immediately.

ZINFANDEL SYRUP

This sauce is particularly delicious over Frozen Zabaglione Ice Cream, *page 43.*

1½ cups red zinfandel wine
½ cup sugar
peeled orange zest of 1 orange
2 tbs. orange juice
½ stick cinnamon
3 whole cloves

Combine ingredients in a small saucepan. Bring to a boil and simmer for about 5 minutes. Strain into a small bowl, cool to room temperature, cover and refrigerate until ready to use.

ICE CREAM ACCOMPANIMENTS

118   Chocolate Biscotti
119   Lemon Almond Biscotti
120   Cookie Cups
122   Lace Cookies
123   Crisp Gingersnaps

   Ice cream and cookies are a classic combination. A cookie or two will provide a nice crunchy counterpoint to cold, creamy ice cream or add a contrasting flavor to a simple sherbet or ice. Cookie cups make an elegant edible dish for ice cream, or you can paint foil cupcake papers with melted chocolate and allow to cool. Peel foil papers off and fill the little cups with a scoop of your favorite ice cream. Cookies make great ice cream sandwiches, too.

CHOCOLATE BISCOTTI

Toasted hazelnuts, walnuts, almonds or pecans are all delicious in this Italian-style cookie.

½ cup unsalted butter, melted	3 large eggs
1 cup sugar	2½ cups all-purpose flour
1 tsp. vanilla extract	3 tbs. unsweetened cocoa
1 tsp. chocolate extract	1½ tsp. baking powder
3 tbs. dark rum or Frangelico	1 cup whole hazelnuts, toasted

Heat the oven to 350°. Mix butter, sugar, vanilla, chocolate extract and rum in a bowl. Whisk eggs and stir into butter-sugar mixture. Sift flour, cocoa and baking powder together and add to bowl, stirring well to combine. Stir in nuts. Form into 2 loaves about 3 inches wide and ¾-inch high on a well-greased or parchment-paper-lined cookie sheet. Bake for 20 to 25 minutes until slightly firm to the touch. Top of loaves may crack. Remove from oven and allow to cool for 5 to 10 minutes. Reduce oven to 300°. Cut loaves into ½-inch slices and place on cookie sheet. Return to oven for about 20 minutes to crisp. Turn cookies over and crisp other side for an additional 15 to 20 minutes. Remove from oven and allow to cool. Store in an airtight container.

NOTE: Toast hazelnuts in a shallow pan in a 350° oven. Shake pan frequently so nuts toast evenly. When nuts start to brown and begin to smell toasty, remove and turn into a rough terry towel. Rub nuts in towel to remove as much brown skin as possible. Cool before adding to dough.

LEMON ALMOND BISCOTTI

Try these with chocolate ice cream or fruit-flavored sherbets.

½ cup unsalted butter, melted
1¼ cups sugar
1 tsp. vanilla extract
1½ tsp. lemon extract
grated zest of 1 lemon

3 tbs. lemon juice
3 eggs
2½ cups all-purpose flour
1 tsp. baking soda
1 cup toasted slivered almonds

Heat the oven to 350°. Combine butter, sugar, vanilla, lemon extract, peel and juice in a mixing bowl. Whisk eggs together and add to butter-sugar mixture. Sift flour and soda together and add to mixing bowl. Stir well to combine. Add almonds. Form into 2 loaves about 3 inches wide and ¾-inch high on a well-greased or parchment-paper-lined cookie sheet. Bake for 20 to 25 minutes until slightly firm to the touch. Tops of loaves may crack. Remove from oven and allow to cool for 5 to 10 minutes. Reduce oven to 300°. Cut loaves into ½-inch slices and place on cookie sheet. Return to oven for about 20 minutes to crisp. Turn cookies over and crisp other side for an additional 15 to 20 minutes. Remove from oven and allow to cool. Store in an airtight container.

COOKIE CUPS

If you are looking for an elegant, easy dessert, serve any wonderful homemade ice cream in these delicate cookie cups. They can be made ahead and kept in an airtight container for a day or two before serving.

1/4 cup butter, room temperature
1/3 cup sugar
1/4 cup egg whites
1/2 tsp. grated lemon zest
1/2 tsp. vanilla extract
1/3 cup sifted all-purpose flour
1 pinch salt

Heat the oven to 400°. Line 2 cookie sheets with parchment paper or foil. Using a 5-inch diameter bowl, trace 2 circles on each sheet. Oil the backs of 2 baking cups or small bowls to be used for forming the cookie cups. In a small bowl, cream butter and sugar together until light and fluffy. Beat in egg whites. Add lemon zest and vanilla. Fold sifted flour and salt into mixture. Using 1 heaping tbs. cookie dough for each cookie cup, place dough in center of marked circles on cookie sheets and spread evenly about $1/8$-inch thick over entire circle. Bake 1 cookie sheet of 2 circles at a time for easier handling. Bake cookies for about 4 to 5 minutes until edges are lightly browned. Remove from oven and slide a large spatula under cookie to lift from cookie sheet. Quickly drape hot cookie over oiled baking cup or bowl. Remove second cookie and form in same manner. If cookies do not seem soft and pliable, return cookie sheet to oven to heat slightly; then form over cups. Continue to bake and mold remaining cookies. Allow to cool. Store in an airtight container until ready to use.

SERVING SUGGESTIONS

Place each cookie cup on a serving plate; fill with 1 or 2 scoops of ice cream and garnish with fresh fruit sauce, sprigs of mint, whipped cream or chocolate shavings.

LACE COOKIES

These crisp, elegant cookies make delicious cookie cups, or you can roll them into cylinders or cone shapes. It is easier to shape them while warm.

1/4 cup light corn syrup
3 tbs. butter
1/3 cup brown sugar
1/2 cup sifted cake flour

1/2 cup toasted finely chopped or ground
   almonds, pecans or walnuts
1 pinch salt

Heat the oven to 325°. Prepare the cookie sheets by oiling or lining with parchment paper. Combine syrup, butter and brown sugar in a small saucepan. Bring to a boil and remove from heat. Stir in flour, nuts and salt. Drop heaping teaspoonfuls of batter onto prepared cookie sheets about 4 inches apart. Bake for 9 to 11 minutes until golden brown. Cool for 1 to 2 minutes and remove from cookie sheets with a wide spatula. Roll into cone shapes or place warm cookies over oiled custard cups or glasses to make cookie cups. Drape cookies over a rolling pin to make cookie tiles. If they are difficult to form, return to oven for a few minutes until they soften. Store these in an airtight container as soon as they have cooled to keep them from absorbing moisture from the air. Reheat briefly in a 300° oven to recrisp if necessary.

CRISP GINGERSNAPS

This old-fashioned, gingery cookie is delicious served beside a dish of ice cream. Form slightly larger cookies to make ice cream sandwiches.

¾ cup shortening or margarine
1 cup sugar, plus 2 tbs.
¼ cup dark molasses
1 egg, lightly beaten
2 cups all-purpose flour

2 tsp. baking soda
1 tsp. ground ginger
1 tsp. cinnamon
½ tsp. ground cloves
1 dash salt

Heat the oven to 350°. Prepare the cookie sheets by oiling or lining with parchment paper. With a mixer, cream shortening and 1 cup sugar until light and fluffy. Add molasses and egg. Mix well. Sift flour, soda, spices and salt. Add to sugar mixture, beating until well combined. Form cookie dough into 1- or 1½-inch diameter balls. Place 2 tbs. sugar on a small plate. Roll cookie balls in sugar. Place on prepared cookie sheets about 2 inches apart. Bake for about 15 minutes until lightly browned. Remove to cooling rack. Store in an airtight container.

OLD-FASHIONED SODA FOUNTAIN TREATS

127   Double Chocolate Malted Milk

127   Maple Malted Milk

128   Root Beer Float

128   Brown Cow

129   Basic Milk Shake

130   Ice Cream Soda

131   Peach Melba Sundae

131   Kir Royale

132   Bellini

132   Strawberries Romanoff Sundae

133   Grasshopper

133   Amaretto Freeze

134   Velvet Hammer

134   Tropical Banana

135   Strawberry Smoothie

135   Peach Cinnamon Delight

136   Pineapple Breeze

136   Mexican Chocolate Cocktail

137   Banana Split

Ice cream specialty stores are noted for serving wonderful cold ice cream sundaes, sodas, floats and banana splits. These can be easily duplicated with delicious homemade ice cream and toppings from the supermarket, or your own sauces.

A make-your-own ice cream or dessert bar is a great way to end a barbecue or summer dinner. Depending on how much time you have, either make or buy the ice cream and toppings. Scoop out several different kinds of ice cream balls ahead of time and keep them in the freezer. Set up the serving area with different ice cream toppings, sauces, sliced fruit and nuts. Put out a plate of homemade cookies, too.

Unusual goblets, tall glasses, pretty glass dishes, long-handled spoons and straws add a festive air to the party.

Some soda fountain tips:

- If you are making a number of servings, make and scoop out the ice cream ahead of time. Place scoops of ice cream on a large, chilled plate and place it in the freezer until serving time.
- Dip the ice cream scoop in warm water between scoops to keep ice cream from sticking.
- Use a regular ice cream dipper for round balls or a spade-type server for oval shapes, or form scoops with a pair of large tablespoons.
- Chill club soda, root beer, fruit juice or other carbonated beverages to be used.
- Use chilled glasses, plates or dishes to avoid instant meltdown.
- Toast nuts for 5 to 10 minutes in a low temperature oven to bring out the flavors.
- Prepare syrups, toppings and nuts, and have whipped cream close at hand for assembling the ice cream creation.
- Fresh raspberries, blueberries, sliced strawberries, peaches or bananas make colorful and tasty accents.

The following recipes are suggested amounts for individual servings and can easily be doubled or tripled as required. Feel free to use your own favorite combinations. If you are serving teenagers or really love ice cream, increase the portion sizes accordingly.

ICE CREAM SUNDAES

Almost every child from the age of 5 knows how to put together a sundae with personal favorite flavors.

A scoop or two of ice cream receives a generous topping of 2 to 3 tbs. flavorful syrup, ice cream topping or sauce. Chopped nuts, whipped cream and maraschino cherries add the final touches.

One of the simplest sundaes is a scoop of ice cream topped with a splash of your favorite after-dinner liqueur.

To make a hot chocolate fudge sundae, heat the chocolate sauce before pouring it over the ice cream. Top with nuts and whipped cream.

The sky is the limit when it comes to creating out-of-this-world sundaes!

ICE CREAM DRINKS

Serve ice cream in the form of an after-dinner drink for an easy, elegant dessert. Many varieties of fruit, coffee, and other flavored liqueurs and brandies are available. Put together your favorite flavors and blend to a creamy finish.

In this chapter are a few classic combinations.

DOUBLE CHOCOLATE MALTED MILK

Servings: 1

Here is a cold, creamy way to satisfy a sweet tooth.

1 cup cold milk
3 tbs. chocolate syrup
1 tbs. malted milk powder

2 large scoops chocolate ice cream
whipped cream for garnish, optional

Place ingredients in a blender and process on HIGH for 30 seconds or until smooth and creamy. Serve in a tall, chilled glass with a straw. Garnish with whipped cream, if desired.

MAPLE MALTED MILK

Servings: 1

Maple syrup makes a delicious malt.

1 cup cold milk
1/4 cup maple syrup
1 tbs. malted milk powder

2 large scoops vanilla ice cream
whipped cream for garnish, optional

Place ingredients in a blender and process on HIGH for 30 seconds or until smooth and creamy. Serve in a tall, chilled glass with a straw. Garnish with whipped cream, if desired.

ROOT BEER FLOAT

Servings: 1

This old-fashioned favorite is a summertime treat. If watching calories, use diet root beer and low-fat ice cream.

chilled root beer

1 large scoop vanilla ice cream

Pour root beer gently down the side of a tall, chilled 12- to 16-ounce glass, allowing room for ice cream. Add ice cream on top; do not stir. Serve with a straw and a long-handled iced tea spoon.

BROWN COW

Servings: 1

This ice cream float is made with a cola instead of root beer.

1/4 cup cold milk
1 tbs. chocolate syrup

chilled cola drink
1 large scoop vanilla ice cream

Combine milk and syrup in a tall, chilled 12- to 16-ounce glass. Stir to combine flavors. Add cola by pouring gently down side of glass to reduce foaming, leaving room for ice cream. Stir gently and add ice cream. Serve immediately with a straw and a long-handled iced tea spoon.

BASIC MILK SHAKE

Use your favorite flavor combinations.

1 cup cold milk
3 tbs. flavored syrup
2 scoops ice cream

Place ingredients in a blender and process on HIGH for about 30 seconds until smooth and creamy. Serve in a tall, chilled glass with a straw.

COMBINATION SUGGESTIONS

- *Raspberry Sauce,* page 113, with strawberry ice cream or frozen yogurt
- butterscotch syrup with vanilla ice cream or *Butterscotch Ice Cream,* page 49
- chocolate syrup with *Mexican Chocolate Ice Cream,* page 31
- *Caramel Sauce,* page 112, with *Creamy Peanut Butter Ice Cream,* page 48

ICE CREAM SODA

The secret to a delicious soda is to serve it while it is still fizzing.

1/4 cup cold milk
2 tbs. flavored syrup
2 scoops ice cream

cold club soda
whipped cream for garnish
maraschino cherry for garnish

Combine milk and flavored syrup and pour into a tall, chilled glass. Add 1 scoop ice cream with a little soda and, using a long-handled spoon, press ice cream into mixture. Add remaining ice cream and fill glass with club soda. Garnish with whipped cream and cherry. Serve immediately with a straw and a long-handled iced tea spoon.

COMBINATION SUGGESTIONS

- raspberry syrup with *Fresh Peach Ice Cream,* page 57
- chocolate syrup with *Coffee Ice Cream,* page 26
- cherry syrup with *Sweet Cherry Ice Cream,* page 39
- strawberry syrup with *Old-Fashioned Lemon Ice Cream,* page 42

PEACH MELBA SUNDAE

Peaches and raspberries are a classic combination.

½ peeled sliced fresh peach, or canned peach
  slices
1 scoop vanilla ice cream
2 tbs. *Raspberry Sauce*, page 113

fresh raspberries for garnish
whipped cream for garnish
sliced almonds for garnish, optional

Place peaches in a small dessert dish, top with ice cream and add *Raspberry Sauce*, page 113. Garnish with fresh raspberries, a dollop of whipped cream and some sliced almonds, if desired.

KIR ROYALE

This is an elegant, light dessert to serve after a formal meal. Use a sweet champagne.

1 scoop *Raspberry Sherbet*, page 76
1 tsp. crème de cassis

⅓ cup champagne
mint sprigs for garnish

Place sherbet in a small, chilled dessert dish. Pour champagne over and top with crème de cassis. Garnish with a sprig of mint. Serve immediately.

BELLINI

Here is an easy dessert. Use a sparkling Italian muscat wine or prosecco.

1 scoop peach sherbet
fresh raspberries

$\frac{1}{3}$ cup Asti Spumante or prosecco

Place sherbet and raspberries in a small goblet or chilled dessert dish. Add sparkling wine and serve immediately.

STRAWBERRIES ROMANOFF SUNDAE

Make this when ripe, juicy strawberries are at their best.

3–4 fresh stemmed sliced strawberries
8–10 fresh raspberries
1 tbs. kirsch or strawberry-flavored liqueur

1 tbs. *Raspberry Sauce,* page 113
1 scoop vanilla ice cream
whipped cream for garnish

Combine strawberries, raspberries, kirsch and *Raspberry Sauce.* Place ice cream in a chilled serving dish. Spoon strawberry mixture over ice cream and top with a little whipped cream. Serve immediately.

GRASSHOPPER

This is a refreshing, minty after-dinner drink.

1 tbs. green crème de menthe
1 tbs. brandy

¾ cup vanilla ice cream

Place ingredients in a blender and process on HIGH until smooth and creamy. Pour into a 6- to 8-ounce wine glass and serve immediately.

AMARETTO FREEZE

Serve one of these instead of dessert.

1 tbs. amaretto
1 tbs. brandy

¾ cup vanilla ice cream

Place ingredients in a blender and process on HIGH until smooth and creamy. Pour into a 6- to 8-ounce wine glass and serve.

VELVET HAMMER

This drink is smooth, creamy and delicious.

1 tbs. crème de cacao
1 tbs. brandy

¾ cup vanilla or chocolate ice cream
½ tsp. vanilla extract

Place ingredients in a blender and process on HIGH until smooth and creamy. Pour into a 6- to 8-ounce wine glass and serve.

TROPICAL BANANA

This is a grand finale for a spicy dinner.

½ ripe banana, thinly sliced
2 tsp. lime juice
1 tbs. dark rum

1 tbs. superfine sugar
¾ cup orange, vanilla or pineapple ice cream

Place ingredients in a blender and process on HIGH until smooth and creamy. Pour into a 6- to 8-ounce wine glass and serve.

STRAWBERRY SMOOTHIE

Strawberries and ice cream make an easy dessert drink.

¼ cup sliced strawberries, fresh or frozen
1 tbs. strawberry syrup

¾ cup vanilla or strawberry ice cream
1 tbs. Triple Sec or orange-flavored liqueur

Place ingredients in a blender and process on HIGH until smooth and creamy. Pour into a 6- to 8-ounce wine glass and serve.

PEACH CINNAMON DELIGHT

This is a cold variation of peaches and cream.

¼ cup sliced fresh or frozen peaches
¾ cup peach or vanilla ice cream
1 pinch cinnamon

1 tbs. light rum
1 tbs. Triple Sec or orange-flavored liqueur

Place ingredients in a blender and process on HIGH until smooth and creamy. Pour into a 6- to 8-ounce wine glass and serve.

PINEAPPLE BREEZE

Servings: 1

This drink features tropical flavors blended with ice cream.

¼ cup canned crushed pineapple
1 tbs. pineapple juice

2 tbs. light rum
¾ cup pineapple or vanilla ice cream

Place ingredients in a blender and process on HIGH until smooth and creamy. Pour into a 6- to 8-ounce wine glass and serve.

MEXICAN CHOCOLATE COCKTAIL

Servings: 1

Cinnamon and chocolate are a classic combination. Serve after a Mexican dinner.

1 tbs. crème de cacao
1 tbs. brandy

¾ cup *Mexican Chocolate Ice Cream*, page 31

Place ingredients in a blender and process on HIGH until smooth and creamy. Pour into a 6- to 8-ounce wine glass and serve.

BANANA SPLIT

A banana split is a total indulgence! Substitute marshmallow sauce for the crushed pineapple if you prefer.

1 banana
lemon juice, optional
1 scoop each chocolate, strawberry and vanilla ice cream
1–2 tbs. chocolate sauce
1–2 tbs. crushed strawberries or strawberry sauce
1–2 tbs. crushed pineapple
finely chopped nuts for garnish
whipped cream for garnish
maraschino cherries for garnish

Split banana in half lengthwise. Brush banana with lemon juice if not using immediately. Place banana halves in a shallow, long dish. Arrange scoops of ice cream on top of banana. Top chocolate ice cream with chocolate sauce, strawberry ice cream with strawberries and vanilla ice cream with pineapple. Sprinkle with nuts and dollops of whipped cream. Place maraschino cherries on last. Serve immediately.

ELEGANT DESSERTS

140   Frozen Lemon Ice Box Pie

141   Key Lime Ice Cream Pie

142   Cookie Crusts

142   Ginger Cookie Crust

143   Graham Cracker Cookie Crust

144   Graham Cracker Nut Crust

145   Ice Cream Cookie Sandwiches and Bars

146   Ice Cream Cake Roll

148   Flaming Strawberries

149   Parfaits

150   Molded Ice Cream Bombes

151   Rainbow Bombe

IDEAS FOR DESSERTS

- Serve scoops of ice cream in small melon or papaya halves and garnish with fresh raspberries, strawberries or blueberries.

- **EASY CHERRIES JUBILEE:** Open a can of pitted Bing cherries with juice and heat in a small saucepan with 2 tbs. brandy. Spoon cherry sauce over dishes of vanilla ice cream.

- An impressive ice cream platter for a crowd or dessert buffet: Scoop out several different flavors of ice cream and sherbet into balls. Place on a chilled platter or serving tray and return to the freezer until party time. Garnish platter with fresh washed lemon tree leaves or fresh mint and scatter fresh berries over tray. Serve with bowls of ice cream sauces, toasted nut and whipped cream.

- Make a dessert pizza using cookie dough for the crust. Bake and cool crust, top with scoops of ice cream, and drizzle a combination of ice cream toppings, nuts and syrups over the ice cream. Cut into wedges to serve. This is popular with the younger crowd.

Desserts involving multiple layers or cake take a little time to put together, so plan to start a day or two before serving the dessert to allow time for freezing each layer before adding the next ingredient. It is important to work as quickly as possible when adding the layers. A quick tip for defrosting ice cream: place plastic or microwaveable container with 2 cups ice cream in microwave and defrost on HIGH for 45 seconds to 1 minute. Repeat defrost for a few more seconds, if needed. Cut the slightly softened ice cream into small thin pieces and spread them in the cake with the back of a spoon or your fingers. If the ice cream is allowed to melt, the texture becomes icy and grainy when it refreezes. Immediately after adding a layer of ice cream, put the dessert back into the freezer and allow the last layer to freeze somewhat firmly before adding another. Sprinkle praline or spoon preserves between layers to add a little texture and flavor contrast. If using liqueurs to flavor an ice cream cake, sprinkle them over the cake before adding the next layer of ice cream.

Frozen ice cream pies will be easier to cut and serve if you wipe the bottom of the pie plate with a towel or sponge dipped in hot water. Dip your knife in hot water and wipe it dry before cutting the individual pie pieces.

FROZEN LEMON ICE BOX PIE

Make your own Graham Cracker Cookie Crust, page 143, or Ginger Cookie Crust, page 142, or buy an already prepared crust from the supermarket. This old time favorite will stand on its own when cut into wedges or just spooned into dishes. Chill prepared crust in the freezer before spooning in filling.

1 can (14 oz.) sweetened condensed milk
grated peel of 1 lemon
1/4 cup fresh lemon juice
1 1/2 cups half-and-half
one 8- or 9-inch cookie crust, chilled

Combine ingredients, except crust, in a blender container or food processor workbowl and blend until smooth. Cover and chill until ready to freeze. Pour into the ice cream maker and follow the manufacturer's instructions for freezing. Spoon softened ice cream into chilled pie crust; smooth top. Lightly cover with plastic wrap and place in the freezer. Remove from freezer and put in the refrigerator to soften about 30 minutes before serving. Cut into wedges and serve.

KEY LIME ICE CREAM PIE

Key lime juice has a very unusual flavor. Some supermarkets carry a bottled Key lime juice, but if unavailable, substitute ¼ cup each lemon juice and regular lime juice. This is good in Graham Cracker Cookie Crust, page 143, or a chocolate cookie crust. The mixture is quite pale, so adding a little food coloring makes a prettier pie. Garnish serving plates with thin lime slices.

1 can (14½ oz.) sweet evaporated milk
⅓ cup (3 oz.) Egg Beaters or egg substitute
½ cup Key lime juice
1 cup half-and-half
few drops green food coloring, optional
one 8- or 9-inch cookie crust, chilled

Combine milk, Egg Beaters, lime juice and half-and-half in a blender container or food processor workbowl. Blend until well combined. Add food coloring if desired. Pour into the ice cream maker and follow the manufacturer's instructions for freezing. Spoon softened ice cream into chilled cookie crust. Smooth top, lightly cover and place in the freezer. Remove from freezer and place in the refrigerator to soften about 30 minutes before serving. Cut into wedges to serve.

COOKIE CRUSTS

Crushed cookie crumbs make wonderful crusts for ice cream pies. Supermarkets have a variety of ready-to-fill cookie crusts as well as boxes of different flavors of cookie crumbs. The prepared cookie crumbs just require a little sugar and melted butter or margarine to assemble and bake. If you like to make your own: buy or bake cookies; crush them and either bake or chill them until firm to keep the crumbs from mixing with the ice cream. Baking produces a slightly more flavorful crust. Homemade crusts can be done ahead, baked and kept in the freezer to be filled on demand. It is important to chill the prepared crust before spooning in the ice cream filling.

GINGER COOKIE CRUST

Makes one 8-inch shell

This crust makes a terrific accompaniment for Spicy Pumpkin Ice Cream, *page 70,* Pumpkin Pecan Ice Cream, *page 71, or* Creamy Peanut Butter Ice Cream, *page 48.*

1 cup (about 5 oz.) finely crushed *Crisp Gingersnaps,* page 123

3 tbs. melted butter
2 tbs. sugar

Combine ingredients, mixing well. Form and bake as directed for *Graham Cracker Cookie Crust,* page 143.

GRAHAM CRACKER COOKIE CRUST

Makes one 9-inch shell

Use a food processor to crush the crackers, or use a rolling pin and crush them between 2 sheets of waxed paper.

1½ cups (about 6 oz.) finely crushed graham cracker crumbs
¼ cup melted butter
3 tbs. brown sugar
⅛ tsp. cinnamon
1 tbs. Triple Sec or orange-flavored liqueur

Heat the oven to 350°. Combine crumbs with butter, sugar and cinnamon, mixing well. Add Triple Sec. Press crumb mixture evenly into a 9-inch pie plate or tart pan. If you have a second pan of the same size, distribute crumbs as evenly as possible in one pan and press second pan on top of crumbs to make a dense, smooth crust. Bake for 8 to 10 minutes, until crust is firm and lightly browned. Remove to a rack. Cool and then chill in the freezer before filling with ice cream.

GRAHAM CRACKER NUT CRUST

Nuts add to the texture and flavor of a basic graham cracker crust.

¾ cup (about 3 oz.) finely crushed graham cracker crumbs
¼ cup melted butter
¼ cup ground toasted walnuts, pecans or almonds
3 tbs. brown sugar

Combine ingredients, mixing well. Form and bake as directed for *Graham Cracker Cookie Crust,* page 143.

ICE CREAM COOKIE SANDWICHES AND BARS

Your favorite cookies, large or small, can be filled with a flavorful ice cream and placed in the freezer for a quick dessert treat for children and adults. Soften the ice cream. Either put it in a pastry bag fitted with a large tip and pipe it onto the flat side of a cookie, or carefully spoon the ice cream over a cookie, topping with another cookie. Use a knife dipped in hot water to smooth the edges and then roll in a garnish of chopped nuts, chocolate bits or toasted coconut. Place in the freezer until firm and then wrap each sandwich in plastic wrap for easy storing.

Consider filling with *Crisp Gingersnaps,* page 123, with *Spicy Pumpkin Ice Cream,* page 70, or *Creamy Peanut Butter Ice Cream,* page 48. Sandwich chocolate cookies with *Easy Caramel Ice Cream, page* 17, *Mexican Chocolate Ice Cream,* page 31, or *Cognac Ice Cream,* page 28.

Mix and bake some cookie dough in an 8-inch square baking pan. Cut into squares and top each square with a scoop of ice cream and a flavor-compatible sauce. Or spread some softened ice cream over the baked, cooled cookie dough; cover and freeze. Cut into squares to serve and top with whipped cream, chocolate sprinkles, toasted coconut or a luscious sauce.

ICE CREAM CAKE ROLL

Ice cream cake rolls make a pretty presentation and can be done ahead of time. Bake the cake a few hours or even a day ahead so there is time to cool for it to cool and chill before filling with softened ice cream. Old Fashioned Lemon Ice Cream, page *42, makes a terrific filling.*

CAKE

4 eggs
1 tsp. baking powder
1/2 tsp. salt
3/4 cup sugar

1 tsp. vanilla
3/4 cup sifted cake flour
powdered sugar

3 cups softened ice cream
1 cup heavy cream, whipped
1/4 cup superfine or powdered sugar

chopped nuts, grated chocolate, flaked
   coconut or instant cocoa mix for garnish

Heat the oven to 375°. Oil a 10-x-15-inch jelly roll pan and line it with parchment or waxed paper. Oil paper liner and lightly dust with flour. Combine eggs, baking powder and salt in a mixer bowl and beat until eggs are thick and lemon colored. Gradually beat in sugar. Add vanilla and fold in flour. Spread batter evenly in prepared pan and bake for 10 to 12 minutes, until lightly browned.

Spread a kitchen towel on the counter; sift a light layer of powdered sugar over towel. Remove cake from oven and turn out on towel. Remove paper liner. Cut off crisp cake edges and gently roll up cake starting with short side, with towel inside the roll. Cool and chill cake in the refrigerator. When ready to fill cake roll, gently unroll cake, remove towel and spread with softened ice cream to within 1/2 inch of edges. Reroll cake and place in the freezer.

Whip heavy cream with 3 tbs. sugar until soft peaks form. Spread over cake roll and sprinkle with desired garnish. Place in refrigerator. As soon as whipped cream has firmed, cover cake with plastic wrap and foil, and freeze for several hours before serving. Place cake in refrigerator about 30 minutes before serving. Cut into slices to serve. Garnish as desired.

VARIATIONS

Sprinkle ice cream layer with 1 cup finely chopped, toasted nuts

Lightly drizzle a few tablespoons strawberry or chocolate ice cream syrup over inside of cake before spreading with ice cream

Spread a thin layer of strawberry, apricot or blackberry preserves over inside of cake before spreading with ice cream.

FLAMING STRAWBERRIES

When making this very elegant dessert, have the ice cream ready in chilled dessert bowls because it only takes a couple of minutes to heat the strawberries. Expand the recipe for the desired number of servings.

1/4 cup orange juice
2 tbs. sugar
1 cup sliced strawberries
3 tbs. brandy
2 scoops vanilla ice cream

Place orange juice and sugar in a small heavy saucepan. Stir over medium heat until sugar dissolves and orange juice has thickened slightly. Add strawberries and heat through. Pour in brandy; allow to heat for a few seconds. Using a fireplace match, carefully flame brandy. Be very careful to avert your face. This should be done under a stove hood or an area where flames will not be in contact with anything flammable. Immediately pour over ice cream in chilled bowls and serve.

PARFAITS

Parfaits are made of layers of ice cream and toppings. They can be done ahead, covered, and kept in the freezer until ready to serve. Use tall parfait glasses or improvise with heavy duty large wine glasses and chill them in the refrigerator or freezer before filling. Part of the charm of this dessert is seeing the contrasting layers. One quart of ice cream will make 4 to 6 servings, depending on the size of the parfait dishes.

PARFAIT IDEAS

- Layer *Apple Cinnamon Sherbet,* page 87, with *Caramel Sauce,* page 112, and ginger cookie or gingerbread crumbs. Garnish with a little whipped cream.

- Layer *Frozen Zabaglione Ice Cream,* page 43, with *Zinfandel Syrup,* page 116, and toasted sliced almonds.

- Layer *Old-fashioned Lemon Ice Cream,* page 42, or *Lemon Cheesecake Ice Cream,* page 62, with *Blueberry Sauce,* page 114, and a few fresh blueberries.

- Layer *Mexican Chocolate Ice Cream,* page 31, with chocolate syrup and chocolate cookie crumbs. Top with a little whipped cream.

- Layer *Pumpkin Pecan Ice Cream,* page 71, with *Caramel Sauce,* page 112, and gingersnap cookie crumbs. Garnish with whipped cream.

MOLDED ICE CREAM BOMBES

Contrasting layers of ice cream or sherbet are packed into an ice cream mold or bowl, frozen, unmolded and sliced into serving portions. The ice cream or sherbet must be softened enough to spread with the back of a spoon. Microwave on DEFROST for 45 to 60 seconds, repeating as necessary for the amount of ice cream you are softening, or place ice cream in the refrigerator for 30 minutes before using. It takes time to create a bombe because each layer must be firmed up in the freezer before the next one is added. It may be more practical to buy some of the ice cream flavors to save time.

A 6-cup mold will make about 8 servings; an 8-cup mold will serve 8 to 10. Chill the mold in the freezer for about 30 minutes before starting.

There are no set rules regarding number of layers or flavor combinations, so use your imagination. One of the layers can be heavy cream whipped with a liqueur, or fresh fruit can be sweetened and folded into the whipped cream. Fruit and nuts can be added to vanilla ice cream to create a special flavor. Unmold and serve as directed on page 151.

Once you have made an ice cream bombe, you will see that the process is quite simple if you allow yourself enough time to do it in easy steps.

RAINBOW BOMBE

This is a four layer delight. Serve it with Zinfandel Syrup, *page 116.*

1 quart *Holiday Eggnog Ice Cream,* page 50,
   or vanilla ice cream mixed with a little dark
   rum and maraschino cherries
1 pint *Pistachio Nut Ice Cream,* page 45

1 pint *Raspberry Sherbet,* page 76
½ cup heavy cream
¼ cup instant cocoa mix

Chill an 8-cup mold in the freezer. Soften eggnog ice cream. Evenly layer the inside of mold with a 1½-inch layer of ice cream, leaving a deep well in the center. Place the mold in the freezer to harden completely, about an hour. When ready to continue soften pistachio ice cream. Make another layer inside mold about ¾-inch thick, leaving a well in the center. Return mold to freezer for another hour. Soften raspberry sherbet. Line mold with a thin even layer of the sherbet. Return mold to freezer for an hour.

Whip heavy cream with cocoa until stiff peaks form. Completely fill center of mold with whipped cream. Cover mold and place in freezer. When ready to serve, quickly dip mold into a bowl filled with hot water for a few seconds, then invert mold over a chilled serving plate. If necessary, apply a hot kitchen towel to mold to get it to release. Cut into wedges with a sharp, hot knife to serve. Pour a thin layer of zinfandel syrup around each piece and serve immediately.

INDEX

A

Almond
  honey ice cream 60
  lemon biscotti 119
  mocha fudge ice cream 24
  praline ice cream 14
Amaretto freeze 133
Apple
  Calvados ice cream 20
  cinnamon sherbet 87
  juice sorbet 99
  quince dairy-free ice cream 63
Apricot frozen yogurt 85
Apricot sauce 111
Avocado spicy ice cream 36

B

Banana
  daiquiri sherbet 92
  nut ice cream 73
  split 137
  tropical 134
Basic milk shake 129
Bellini 132
Biscotti, chocolate 118
Biscotti, lemon almond 119
Bittersweet chocolate mocha sorbet 93
Blackberry frozen yogurt 81
Blackberry rhubarb ice cream 55
Blood orange sorbet 100
Blueberry sauce 114

Blueberry sherbet 78
Bombe, rainbow 151
Bombes, molded, about 150
Bourbon in dulce de leche ice cream 27
Brandy
  and prune frozen yogurt 80
  in Amaretto freeze 133
  in apple Calvados ice cream
  in apricot sauce 111
  in cognac ice cream 28
  in flaming strawberries 148
  in grasshopper 133
  in hazelnut gelato 19
  in holiday eggnog ice cream 50
  in Irish coffee ice cream 23
  in Mexican chocolate cocktail 136
  in Mexican chocolate sauce 115
  in velvet hammer 134
Brown cow cocktail 128
Butter pecan rich ice cream 38
Buttermilk chocolate ice cream 95
Buttermilk tangerine ice cream 59
Butterscotch ice cream 49
Butterscotch sauce 111

C

Cake, ice cream roll 146
Calvados apple ice cream 20
Caramel
  easy ice cream 17
  quick sauce 113

  sauce 112
Carrot, savory freeze 90
Cherry
  chocolate ice cream 40
  dried ice cream 56
  jubilee 138
  sweet ice cream 39
Chestnut rum ice cream 44
Chocolate
  biscotti 118
  bittersweet mocha sorbet 93
  buttermilk ice cream 95
  cherry ice cream 40
  creamy frozen yogurt 68
  double malted milk 127
  gelato 21
  German's pecan ice cream 30
  Mexican cocktail 136
  Mexican ice cream 31
  Mexican sauce 115
  old-fashioned ice cream 33
  orange ice cream 18
  pecan praline ice cream 16
  rocky road ice cream 35
  sugar-free ice cream 94
  super ice cream 34
  white, coconut gelato 22
Cinnamon apple sherbet 87
Cinnamon candy ice cream 66
Coconut orange sherbet 46
Coconut white chocolate gelato 22

Coffee ice cream 26
Coffee, Irish ice cream 23
Cognac ice cream 28
Cookie crusts, about 142
Cookie cups 120
Cranberry orange sorbet 101
Cream sherry ice cream 67
Creamy chocolate frozen yogurt 68
Creamy peanut butter ice cream 48
Crisp gingersnaps 123
Crust
 ginger cookie 142
 graham cracker cookie 143
 graham cracker nut 144
Custard, rich vanilla ice cream 53

D
Dairy-free
 apple juice sorbet 99
 bittersweet chocolate mocha sorbet 93
 blood orange sorbet 100
 cranberry orange sorbet 101
 dried peach sorbet 84
 dried pear sorbet 102
 fresh plum sorbet 103
 orange spiced tea sherbet 104
 pink grapefruit sorbet 105
 quince apple ice cream 63
 rum raisin ice cream 77
 strawberry balsamic sorbet 75
 strawberry daiquiri ice 107
 watermelon sorbet 109
Double chocolate malted milk 127
Dried apricot frozen yogurt 85
Dried cherry ice cream 56

Dried peach sorbet 84
Dried pear sorbet 102
Dulce de leche ice cream 271

E
Easy caramel ice cream 17
Easy chocolate malted ice cream 69
Eggnog holiday ice cream 50

F
Flaming strawberries 148
Float, brown cow 128
Float, root beer 128
Fresh peach ice cream 57
Fresh pineapple sorbet 79
Fresh plum sorbet 103
Frozen lemon ice box pie 140
Frozen yogurt
 blackberry 81
 creamy chocolate 68
 dried apricot 85
 prune and brandy 80
 strawberry 83
 vanilla 72
Frozen zabaglione ice cream 43
Fudge, almond mocha ice cream 24

G
Gazpacho ice 89
Gelato
 chocolate 21
 hazelnut 19
 white chocolate coconut 22
German's chocolate pecan ice cream 30

Ginger
 in savory carrot freeze 90
 papaya sherbet 58
 pineapple ice cream 65
 two- ice cream 29
Ginger cookie crust 142
Gingersnaps, crisp 123
Goat cheese, honey ice cream 25
Graham cracker cookie crust 143
Graham cracker nut crust 144
Grapefruit, pink sorbet 105
Grasshopper 133
Green tea Matcha ice cream 32

H
Hazelnut gelato 19
Holiday eggnog ice cream 50
Honey almond ice cream 60
Honey goat cheese ice cream 25

I
Ice cream cake roll 146
Ice cream drinks 126
Ice cream ingredients 2–9
Ice cream makers 8
Ice cream soda 130
Irish coffee ice cream 23

K
Key lime ice cream pie 141
Kir royale 131
Kiwi orange sherbet 86

L

Lace cookies 122
Lemon
   almond biscotti 119
   cheesecake ice cream 62
   frozen ice box pie 140
   old-fashioned ice cream 42
   tea ice cream 64

M

Malted
   double chocolate milk 127
   easy chocolate ice cream 69
   maple milk 127
Mango orange sherbet 88
Maple malted milk 127
Maple pecan ice cream 97
Matcha, green tea ice cream 32
Mexican chocolate
   cocktail 136
   ice cream 31
   chocolate sauce 115
Milk shake, basic 129
Mocha
   almond fudge ice cream 24
   bittersweet chocolate sorbet 93
   sherbet 96
Molded bombes, about 150

N

Nut banana ice cream 73
Nut graham cracker crust 144

O

Old-fashioned chocolate ice cream 33
Old-fashioned lemon ice cream 42
Orange
   blood, sorbet 100
   chocolate ice cream 18
   coconut sherbet 46
   cranberry sorbet 101
   kiwi sherbet 86
   mango sherbet 88
   spiced tea sherbet 104
   walnut ice cream 61

P

Papaya ginger sherbet 58
Parfaits, about 149
Peach
   cinnamon delight 135
   dried sorbet 84
   fresh ice cream 57
   in bellini 132
   melba sundae 131
Peanut brittle ice cream 47
Peanut butter, creamy ice cream 48
Pear, dried sorbet 102
Pecan
   chocolate praline ice cream 16
   German's chocolate ice cream 30
   maple ice cream 97
   pumpkin ice cream 71
   rich butter ice cream 38
   in rocky road ice cream 35
Philadelphia-style vanilla ice cream 52
Pie, frozen lemon ice box 140

Pie, key lime ice cream 141
Pineapple
   breeze 136
   fresh sorbet 79
   ginger ice cream 65
   sherbet 91
Pink grapefruit sorbet 105
Pistachio nut ice cream 45
Plum, fresh sorbet 103
Praline almond ice cream 14
Praline chocolate pecan ice cream 16
Prune and brandy frozen yogurt 80
Pumpkin pecan ice cream 71
Pumpkin, spicy ice cream 70

Q

Quick caramel sauce 113
Quince apple dairy-free sherbet 63

R

Rainbow bombe 151
Raspberry
   in bellini 132
   sauce 113
   sherbet 76
   vanilla swirl ice cream 51
Rhubarb
   blackberry ice cream 55
   strawberry frozen yogurt 82
   sherbet 106
Rocky road ice cream 35
Roll, ice cream cake 146
Root beer float 128

Rum
  chestnut ice cream 44
  in banana daiquiri sherbet 92
  in chocolate biscotti 118
  in dulce de leche ice cream 27
  in Mexican chocolate sauce 115
  in peach cinnamon delight 135
  in pineapple breeze 136
  in pumpkin pecan ice cream 71
  in strawberry daiquiri ice 1071
  in tropical banana 134
  raisin dairy-free ice cream 77

S
Sandwiches and bars, about 144
Sauce(s)
  apricot 111
  blueberry 114
  butterscotch 111
  caramel 112
  Mexican chocolate 115
  quick caramel 113
  raspberry 113
  zinfandel syrup 116
Savory
  carrot freeze 90
  gazpacho ice 89
  spicy avocado ice cream 36
Sherbet
  apple cinnamon 87
  banana daiquiri 92
  blueberry 78
  kiwi orange 86
  mango orange 88
  mocha 96

orange coconut 46
orange spiced tea 104
papaya ginger 58
pineapple 91
raspberry 76
rhubarb 106
strawberry guava nectar 108
Sherry, cream ice cream 67
Soda, ice cream 130
Sorbet
  apple juice 99
  bittersweet chocolate mocha 93
  blood orange 100
  cranberry orange 101
  dried peach 84
  dried pear 102
  fresh plum 103
  pink grapefruit 105
  strawberry balsamic 75
  watermelon 109
Spicy avocado ice cream 36
Spicy pumpkin ice cream 70
Strawberry
  balsamic sorbet 75
  daiquiri ice 107
  flaming 148
  frozen yogurt 83
  guava nectar sherbet 108
  rhubarb frozen yogurt 82
  rich ice cream 37
  Romanoff sundae 132
  smoothie 135
Sugar-free chocolate ice cream 94
Sundae, peach melba 131
Sundae, strawberries Romanoff 132

Super chocolate ice cream 34
Sweet cherry ice cream 39

T
Tangerine buttermilk ice cream 59
Tropical banana 134
Two ginger ice cream 29

V
Vanilla
  frozen yogurt 72
  Philadelphia-style ice cream 52
  raspberry swirl ice cream 51
  rich custard ice cream 53
Velvet hammer 134

W
Walnut orange ice cream 61
Watermelon sorbet 109
Whiskey, in Irish coffee ice cream 23
White chocolate coconut gelato 22

Y
Yogurt, drained 7
Yogurt, vanilla frozen 72

Z
Zabaglione, frozen ice cream 43
Zinfandel syrup 116

Serve Creative, Easy, Nutritious Meals with **nitty gritty**® Cookbooks

1 or 2, Cooking for
100 Dynamite Desserts
9 x 13 Pan Cookbook
Asian Cooking
Bagels, Best
Barbecue Cookbook
Beer and Good Food
Big Book Bread Machine
Big Book Kitchen Appliance
Big Book Snack, Appetizer
Blender Drinks
Bread Baking
New Bread Machine Book
Bread Machine III
Bread Machine V
Bread Machine VI
Bread Machine, Entrees
Burger Bible
Cappuccino/Espresso
Casseroles
Chicken, Unbeatable
Chile Peppers
Cooking in Clay

Coffee and Tea
Convection Oven
Cook-Ahead Cookbook
Crockery Pot, Extra-Special
Deep Fryer
Dehydrator Cookbook
Dessert Fondues
Edible Gifts
Edible Pockets
Fabulous Fiber Cookery
Fondue and Hot Dips
Fondue, New International
Freezer, 'Fridge, Pantry
Garlic Cookbook
Grains, Cooking with
Healthy Cooking on Run
Ice Cream Maker
Indoor Grill, Cooking on
Irish Pub Cooking
Italian, Quick and Easy
Juicer Book II
Kids, Cooking with Your
Kids, Healthy Snacks for

Loaf Pan, Recipes for
Low-Carb
No Salt No Sugar No Fat
Party Foods/Appetizers
Pasta Machine Cookbook
Pasta, Quick and Easy
Pinch of Time
Pizza, Best
Porcelain, Cooking in
Pressure Cooker
Rice Cooker
Salmon Cookbook
Sandwich Maker
Simple Substitutions
Slow Cooking
Slow Cooker, Vegetarian
Soups and Stews
Soy & Tofu Recipes
Tapas Fantásticas
Toaster Oven Cookbook
Waffles & Pizzelles
Wedding Catering book
Wraps and Roll-Ups

"Millions of books sold—for more than 35 years" **For a free catalog, call: Bristol Publishing Enterprises
(800) 346-4889
www.bristolpublishing.com**